D0269466

⭑ The ⭑
RORY'S
STORIES
GUIDE to the GAA

Rory O'Connor

Gill Books

Gill Books
Hume Avenue
Park West
Dublin 12
www.gillbooks.ie

Gill Books is an imprint of M.H. Gill & Co.

978 07171 7925 1

Illustrations by Jen Murphy
Copy-edited by Seirbhísí Leabhar
Proofread by Emma Dunne
Printed by ScandBook AB, Sweden

This book is typeset in Minion Pro 12/17 pt.

The paper used in this book comes from the wood pulp of
managed forests. For every tree felled, at least one tree is
planted, thereby renewing natural resources.

A CIP catalogue record for this book is available from the
British Library.

Contents

GAA legends

Epilogue   219

Introduction

Back in November 2013, when I decided to start 'Rory's Stories', GAA videos weren't on my mind, to be honest. I've always had a passion for becoming an actor, comedian and entertainer, but finding a niche is the toughest challenge, because it's hard to stand out from the crowd in that game, with so many other people creating content.

In January 2014 I was training with my club, Donaghmore-Ashbourne, on a Sunday morning. I asked a friend of mine, Trevor O'Neill, if he'd mind coming down to the dressing-room after training that morning to film a clip for me. He obliged, thank God.

After the training session I asked some of my team-mates to come into the empty dressing-room, and I handed them each a club jersey. They didn't really have much of a clue what was going on: they always knew I was stone mad, but this was a different level, as far as they were concerned.

'Right, lads,' I told them, 'I'm going to film a sketch of a typical rant by a club manager at half time in a county final. All youse have to do is sit there and look a bit down—just imagine we're in a county final and we're down by seven points, playing absolutely shite.'

Once I had them all in place I stormed into the dressing-room—wearing a big stupid-looking hat, a pair of glasses, a pair of socks pulled up to the knees, and with a bainisteoir bib wrapped around me—and went on a complete rant, 100 per cent off the cuff. I said all sorts of stuff you'll hear at half time in every county final all over the country.

'Ye haven't showed up yet.'

'You're standing around with yer fingers up yer holes admiring the crowd.'

'Johnny, stop looking up into the stand wondering if yer missus is watching ya. Get yourself into this game.'

'If we win, men, I can guarantee you we will drink and have the craic for a month.'

'Leave everything on the field in the second half— no regrets.'

'Now get out there and show some pride in the jersey.'

And I bollocked a few players about not marking their men tight enough, etc., etc. I posted it online that day, and within twenty-four hours it had 30,000 views. Holy shite, I thought to myself. Then it got picked up by popular Irish internet sites, like Joe.ie and Balls.ie. So the penny dropped: I realised that nobody had really gone in-depth into comedy about the GAA.

It still baffles me that the niche was wide open for so long, considering that the GAA is full of messers and characters. The likes of the D'Unbelievables and Dermot Morgan (RIP) had touched on it, but nobody went to the grass roots and showed what really goes on in every club and at every match throughout the country. With social media constantly on the rise, I realised that this was my chance to get my name out there. So for the following six months I went hammer and tongs making GAA sketches.

People might think I have a big production team behind me, filming these sketches, but if the truth be told I film and edit the majority of them on my mobile phone. Genius or cowboy, I don't know—I can let you decide that for yourself—but I feel that the rawness is what makes the sketches come across as real life: no real scripts, just acting out what I've witnessed at one stage or another at GAA matches.

I remember writing down every single player, character and topical moment and person in the GAA I've come across over the years and getting down to work. During the summer of 2014 we were filming three sketches every Saturday and posting them on Facebook during the week. The 'likes' on my page were snowballing: on average, I was getting a thousand followers a day. Madness!

I wasn't willing to rest on my laurels and let someone else come along in the same niche market, so I just went at it flat out until the ideas started to get harder to come by. By then, the following was at more than 100,000, so in my eyes the platform was built: I just had to keep producing the sketches.

As you can imagine, we have some mighty craic filming. I don't have a crew, really: I just beg lads to come down and help. Big Paddy Murphy has always been the reliable one for me—a great help over the years, and a naturally funny man with a good comic brain. He was around from the very early days, helping me out with the videos. A lot of my friends have appeared in them, along with my father, Joe; my mother, Marie; my sister Carol—and even my daughter Ella!

You couldn't meet a bigger GAA man than me, and I have real passion for the comedy side of things. I'm honoured that I've been given the chance to show the GAA world that every club in Ireland is the exact same: the interaction following the Facebook videos proves that every club has the same characters.

When I was given the opportunity by Gill Books to write this book I was delighted. I feel it explains everything you need to know about the amazing organisation that is the GAA. If you play it yourself, I guarantee you that when you read about some of the characters I portray you will know someone in your club just like it. If you have no clue whatsoever who I'm on about, well, there's a very good chance that you are that person.

I hope you enjoy the book.

The beginning of the GAA to now

The beginning

On 1 November 1884 seven men got together in Hayes Hotel in Thurles to form the Gaelic Athletic Association. Who could have predicted the effect that this meeting would have on the future and the culture of the Irish people? Fast forward 133 years and GAA is the most popular sport in Ireland. Every parish and town you pass through will have a GAA field. It's now played in more than thirty countries, from Thailand to Denmark and from New Zealand to France, and it's often a great foundation for Irish people to make friends abroad. Join the local GAA club, get hooked up with a good job and have drinking buddies at the weekend. I think it's fair to say that you'll find welcoming arms in any GAA club around the world, carrying on the great tradition of friendship and respect.

How to explain GAA to non-Irish people

GAA is as rare a sport as some of the characters involved in it. Have you ever been abroad, watching a match in some Irish pub, with a few non-Irish people there, and they ask you what game that is on the telly? You feel like saying, 'How long have ya got!'

Imagine you're on a cruise ship somewhere in the Caribbean, having a few beers with a fella from America, and he says to you, 'Hey, uh, this sport you guys have called, uh, Gaelic games ... What's involved in that? Looks pretty awesome.'

How in the name of Jaysus do ya even begin to explain everything that is Gaelic games. You'd be better off printing off the below information and carrying it around in your wallet. Any time the question is brought up, just hand them the information and then stand back for a blizzard of questions.

Here is the GAA explained as straight down the middle as possible. The association covers men's football and hurling, as well as handball and rounders, and there is also women's football and hurling (camogie). For the games of football and hurling:

- every parish in Ireland has a GAA club;
- there are fifteen players on each team;
- you get 3 points for a goal; if it goes over the bar and between the posts you get 1 point;
- they are not professional sports, but players can train up to seven days a week for their

team and play in front of more than 80,000 people;

- you play for your club first, then for your county, against all other counties, to determine who the all-Ireland champions will be;

- if you win a final you drink for seven days; if you lose a final you drink for seven days;

- fellas you went to school with but who are from a different club—these you hate, and you want to beat them the most;

- you could play at the lowest level possible and still be expected not to go on holidays all year and to stick to drink bans;

- if you move to another club, or even support one, it is highly frowned on, and some older people might never talk to you again;

- if you get injured playing for your club it can take up to a lifetime to get your money back from the insurance.

I accept no further questions, your honour!

My top 5 memories playing underage GAA

I grew up playing GAA in the early 90s, when training consisted only of matches and shooting, with everyone just running around after the ball. No tactics, positions or structures: just a bunch of young lads mad for a bit of craic. Here are some of my best memories of playing at the underage level.

1. Being able to run all day

What is it about being so fit when you play underage? You could play two matches a day, not a bother. I don't even think you sweat at under-14. Can anyone even remember being tired? No warm-up, no warm-down, no stretching, just flat-out from the first whistle to the last, then home in the gear, dirty grass-stained knees, bag flung on the floor, and leap-frog up onto the couch to watch cartoons, before the spuds are put out in front of you. Shower about two hours later. Wake up the next day, zero stiffness in the body, another two matches that day, and off you go. Aw, to be twelve again!

2. Meeting before the game

The under-10 days are probably your most enjoyable. You all meet before the game, sprint out of your parents' car and form a group, laughing and kicking or pucking around. Then you split up into cars to head off.

No fewer than six young bodies get into an auld Toyota, and off you go—doing the driver's head in asking a hundred questions en route to the game.

'Turn up the radio.'

'Change the channel.'

'What team are we playing today?'

'How do I put down this window?'

'Can we stop in the shop?'

'I feel a bit car-sick. Can you pull over, please?'

3. Arriving at the pitch

As you arrive, everyone bails out of the cars, and more often than not you get togged out behind the goals or on the side of the pitch. No warm-up, no stretching, just straight into the game. Managers, who more than likely have a son or daughter on the team, do their best to try and explain some sort of tactics, but ya may as well be talking to the corner flag!

I had an old manager, a solid Corkman, who had this saying any time you questioned him: 'No ifs, no buts, just let the ball do the work.' He'd often hold the ball in his hands and say, 'Go find me a man who can run quicker than this ball can travel with a good kick!' and he'd boot the ball forty yards down the field. 'Exactly. Now I don't want to see any hops or solos: just kick it as far as you can, every time.'

To be fair to him, it was solid tactics. Sure look at football nowadays: so many games are dominated by the hand-pass. Lads are afraid to kick the ball in case they give away possession. It's healthy going to watch an under-10 or under-12 game where the player's first thought when they receive the ball or sliotar is to drive it as far as they can towards their opponent's goal. 'That's the ball, Mickey. Drive it as far as you can, good man.'

4. Being asked to play for the other team

Everyone has played in underage games where one team is short a body or two, and you could be the unfortunate player the manager approaches before throw-in. 'Listen, Rory, the other team is down a couple of bodies, so if we want to make our journey here today worthwhile we have to give them two players. So we're going to give them yourself and John—not because you aren't our best players, but we have to give them decent lads ...' What he really means is, you won't benefit the other team whatsoever, so we're sure to win. But you're a brave man if you say that to a ten-year-old.

So, once you're picked, off you go into the far dressing-room, away from your buddies and over to the dark side. You slowly enter the dressing-room, where nobody knows you. There's a cagey atmosphere as you're handed your jersey.

You'll be in one of three positions. The first is goalie, which is horrific: it's bad enough you got the short straw and have to play with the other team, but now you don't even play outfield. You have to stand in the net as your team-mates and school buddies hammer goal after goal past you! If you're not in goals you'll be either corner-back or corner-forward, where there's a good chance you won't touch the ball for the entire game.

The only thing you can be thankful for is that you didn't take Mammy's advice and put your vest on that morning.

'Rory, Rory ...'

'*What*, Ma?'

'Put a vest under your T-shirt. You'll catch your death in that weather.'

'No, Ma. I'll be grand.'

'Fine, then. Don't come crying to me when you have a head cold. I warned you!'

You would gladly take a head cold any day of the week over having to unveil a Dunnes Stores vest to a bunch of young lads you'd never met before. You'd be off on the wrong foot straight away! If you're lucky, one or two fellas on the team might come up and welcome you in the dressing-room, but young lads can be little bolloxes at times and will more than likely leave you sitting in the corner as they laugh and have the banter among themselves.

You'll sit there with your arms folded, pissed off with your manager for throwing you to the wolves, and your new manager for the day will say, 'Right, lads, settle down for a second. Sorry, what's your name again?' as he looks over at you.

'Eh, Rory.'

'Lads, Rory is going to be our goalkeeper today.' As the jersey is slung in your direction, hitting you in the face, you think, That's it. I'm going to rugby next week!

5. Heading home

When the game is over, and with the score-line reading 4-2 to 5-1, you hop back into the car and head for home. One thing is certain: you will harass the driver.

'Can we stop in the shop, please?'

'No.'

'Can we stop in the shop, please?'

'No.'

'Can we *pleeease* stop in the shop?'

'All right, all right. Give me strength ...'

So in pulls the car for the legendary combination of TK or Score orange and a packet of Tayto crisps.

Everyone's fondest memories of their glory days playing underage GAA: arriving home with dirty knees to the mother, with your rosy red head, a half-empty backwashed bottle of TK and breath banging of cheese and onion. Great times!

My memory of being introduced to hurling

The GAA is a serious tradition in Ireland: like it or lump it, the first sport you'll most likely play as a nipper is GAA, and in nearly all counties it will be hurling and football, number 1. Most auld lads would describe soccer as the 'foreign sport'.

I remember the day I played hurling for the first time. I was no older than seven, and it was a lovely summer's evening—freshly cut grass on the pitch, nettles all along the side, just waiting to pounce on a young lad who'd over-hit a sliotar!

When I got to the pitch I gave my name and was handed a hurl, and we were told to spread out forty yards and puck the sliotar to each other. This seemed to come very natural to everyone around me, but I was a typical young townie used to playing soccer around by the shops, where the craic was that whoever had jumpers on had to sacrifice them as goalposts—the great days!

Well, I was finding the going very tough, making at least two 'fresh airs' before I even connected with the sliotar. Even when I did connect, God knows how far the ball would travel: one would go off over a lad's head, and the other would skim off the stick and go about seven yards in front of me. Very rusty, to say the least.

This went on for a while, before we were called into a huddle by our manager, Big John. 'Mooney', we called him, and he was the biggest brute of a man you can imagine. He was from the heart of Co. Kilkenny and had a voice that would scare the bejaysus out of you. He had a pair of hands on him like two big frying-pans, and he had never been seen with a clean pair of trousers on him. A very raw man, but a gent.

'Right, lads,' he says, 'we have a few new boys joining the team today: Rory, Colin and Philip. Welcome, lads ...' We would have been considered the 'bold boys' at school, so a few lads were a bit intimidated by our showing up.

Mooney turned round and says, 'Right, men, I need to find a goalie. Who wants to play in goals?' Of course, nobody put their hand up: sure, for the love of God, who wants to be a goalie in hurling—only the maddest of the mad survive between the sticks on a hurling pitch! 'Okay, so, I'll do it my way,' says Mooney, and he picked out the three biggest lads in the group. I was one of them. 'Right, chaps,' says he, 'we have to find a goalie for this team, so I need to test ye out.'

Holy God, what does he mean by that, I said to myself, as I looked on with a dog shit of a hurl in my hand and a Celtic jersey on me.

So this lad named Mark was up first—a big, tall, gangly gossoon with a pair of shin pads on him and a raggedy auld Wexford jersey on his back.

Mooney stands about fifteen yards out from goals with a goalie's shovel in his hand and three sliotars at his feet. 'Right, boys, I'll hit three balls at ye each, and whoever saves the most is our goalie. It's as simple as that!'

Holy Mother of God, he can't be serious, I thought, as I stood in line, already starting to regret beginning a hurling career.

So Mooney flicked up the first sliotar with his hurl and absolutely launched it at poor auld Mark, who dived out of the way. Mooney ate the head off him. 'Lord *Jaysus*, gossoon, you're meant to save the ball, not jump out of the way.' Mark did the same with the next two balls. 'Right, Mark, well, it's safe to say you won't be our goalie. Stand aside there.'

Then up stepped Tommy. Mooney did the exact same to him. 'God, lads, have we any goalies at all! Did ye ever see Davy Fitz jump out of the way of the ball? Never! Bunch of pansies I have here ...' And we all ten years of age and under, with barely a hair on our legs!

'Right, in goals there with ya, Rory.' I was shitting it altogether. I had bad asthma and could feel my chest tighten with nerves. Here I was at my first hurling training session, and I was being asked to stand in front of a beast of a man with a massive hurl in his hands, and I was expected to save the sliotars he was going to launch at my head!

I managed to jump out of the way of the first two, but I wasn't so lucky with the last one! It caught me right on my shin bone. 'Ow, me shin!' I shouted as I dived onto the ground.

Mooney stood there with a big grin on his face and says, 'Right, young O'Connor, you'll be the goalie, so!'

After that mini-nightmare was over it only got worse. Mooney had us in groups of four, pulling the shins off each other for the next fifteen minutes, all the while shouting at us, 'I'm telling ye, men, this might be sore now, but your legs will learn to get used to wild pulls, so we'll be more than ready when we come across a dirty shower from north Meath!'

When that bit of torture was over we spent the last fifteen minutes trying to puck the ball over the bar, every one of us absolutely bolloxed from pulling the shins off each other. The session ended soon after that, and we all gathered round the back of Mooney's work van, where he handed us a bottle of Score and a bag of Tayto.

'There ya go, young chaps—great session. 'Twill be the same again next Tuesday evening.'

That's the way it was back then, and it was great. Nowadays everything has gone a bit too much 'health and safety', if ya ask me. I wouldn't change the way I was introduced to the small-ball game. Characters like Big John Mooney are what shape you, and they have made the GAA what it is today.

The characters on every club team

If there's one thing I've learnt making 'Rory's Stories' sketches it's that every GAA club team all over the world has the exact same characters. There might be a guy on your team who you look at during training and matches, and you think to yourself, Look at the head on that lad: he has to be a one-off. In fact, you couldn't be more wrong. Every club has that player. Here are the most common types on every club team.

The dirty corner-back

This man prides himself on making the lives of cocky corner-forwards a misery. This is the type of player you want in your corner.

Most hurlers and footballers pray for a lovely, dry day—for quick hands, quick feet and a good free-flowing game. Not the dirty corner-back. No, you'll find him lying in bed on a championship morning. You could find him sleeping on a bed with no sheet or pillow. He probably sleeps bollock-naked, with only a pair of black socks on him, and those with holes at the tip, and he'll have his toes, with long, dirty nails, sticking out. *Raw!* He lives on a diet of porridge, spuds and Smithwick's.

He'll get anything up to five years out of the one pair of boots. He'll wear no gloves on a pissy, wet day. He might not kick a ball in sixty minutes, but he could still get man of the match for completely ruining the day of the opposition's chief marksman. And he's a great man for breaking hurls during a match.

These boys don't say too much: that's what's frightening about them. They stand over your shoulder for nearly the whole game and just breathe on you, their body language as much as saying, If you run for the next ball I'll take your head clean off your shoulders.

They rarely have good dress sense: baggy jeans, horrible auld shirts and a pair of plain-as-day black or brown shoes. These fellas are not ones for the nightclubs or the Jägerbombs.

The GAA has had plenty of these players over the years. In football you had Francie Bellew of Armagh—a man you simply don't mess with—and Ryan 'Ricey' McMenamin of Tyrone. No-nonsense men. On the hurling front you had Diarmuid 'the Rock' O'Sullivan of Cork, who struck fear into everyone, and JJ Delaney of Kilkenny. He fits the bill: a man who takes no prisoners.

If you are to have a successful team you most certainly need a couple of dirty corner-backs in your starting fifteen.

The cocky corner-forward

Definitely the most-disliked man on any team. He thinks he's the hero, the main man, the best-looking, the best player and the go-to guy. He prides himself on kicking handy frees or pucking over sliotars from all angles of the field as he swaggers back into the corner.

On the pitch he'll be wearing a pair of size-32 shorts on a big 38-inch arse, and a pair of white boots. He has his hair gelled and has white tape round his wrists (even though he's never made a tackle in his life). He's the type of lad who takes two minutes over a fourteen-yard free straight in front of goals; he picks up some grass to check for wind, even on an extremely calm day. He goes through his routine, and on his second or third step back he'll say to himself, I am *class*.

Once the ball is kicked over the black spot at the centre of the crossbar, or wide, he straight away starts pointing and shouting at the rest of the forwards, 'Mark up, mark up!' This sickens everyone else on the field, and you feel like shouting over, '*You* fucking mark up. You've done nothing all game but kick handy frees and roar and shout at everyone, so shut up and start putting in some tackles.'

After the matches he can be seen at the bar in a €200 shirt buttoned up to the top button, almost choking himself, with a pair of jeans painted onto him and a pair of shiny brown pointed boots that look more like a pair of fancy bowling shoes. More than likely he won't have any socks on. He'll be standing there sipping on a bottle of WKD Blue or Corona waiting for the die-hards to come up and shake his hand.

'Well done, Johnny. Great game. Some mighty frees.'

'Cheers, Mac. It was a great team effort: the lads around me were unreal.'

But in his own mind he's saying, 'Of course, *I* was unreal. Sure I *am* this club. Without me youse'd be a useless team. I am the king.'

I can guarantee you that, after a good performance, this fella will be waiting down the newsagent's to pick up the local paper and read about himself, craving the headline 'Johnny is the hero ...'

He won't even see anyone else's name as he glides through the match report seeking praise for his own display. He'll meet lads at training the following Tuesday and be greeted with 'Ya got a fair write-up in the paper, Johnny.'

'Really? Didn't see it, to be honest ...'

Be no hope of him buying the paper if he has a poor outing and the team are beat—zero chance!

Every team in the country has this lad. Not a man you'd be bringing to the trenches with you, but I suppose he's a kind of 'can't live with, can't live without' type of player.

The lad on every team who gives 100 per cent but never gets a game

Every team has its various characters; a team wouldn't be a team without different personalities. We all know the fella who'd go through a wall for you. Never misses training. In fact, he could be up half an hour early,

Right Danny, warm up there!

THE LAD ON EVERY TEAM WHO GIVES 100%
BUT NEVER GETS A GAME

helping the manager line out the cones. He'll be licking the manager's arse to give himself a slight chance of a game on the Sunday.

He's the one man who's guaranteed not to miss training all year. The only issue is that he wouldn't be the most talented player you'd have come across. Below is a list of credentials that will fit the bill. He will:

- be head-to-toe in the correct club gear and never be seen in different togs or socks;

- be an extremely proud clubman;

- be always first to training;

- not have made the starting fifteen since he was under-12s;

- wear a gumshield 24/7;

- have the best of football boots (up to six pairs);

- have dozens of pairs of gloves, a new pair nearly every training session;

- have under-armour shorts on all season long.

Each weekend, when he'd arrive for the match—again, up to twenty minutes before the rest of the team—he'd be togged out, boots on, club raincoat zipped up to the top, and be raring to go. When the starting fifteen is named, and the subs, he is, as usual, number 27 on the programme; he'd have a big, bulling thick head on him. He'd sit on the bench, almost hopping off it with enthusiasm, waiting for that monumental moment when the manager turns to the bench, makes eye contact with him and shouts, 'Right, Danny, warm up there!' Danny would jump up from the bench the way others leap off the couch when the mother shouts 'Dinner's ready' on Christmas Day!

Danny will sprint up and down the sideline like a lunatic, doing all sorts of crazy stretches. He'll go into overdrive when he sees a selector writing out the sub docket for him, and he'll have a little pep talk with himself. 'This is it, Danny boy. This is your chance to show everyone how good you are. You're flying fit: just hit the first man who moves, and when you get the ball go for a point straight away.'

But, ya see, what happens is that the manager gets carried away with the on-field action, most of the time, and before they know it the final whistle has blown, and poor Danny is left standing there on the sideline hopping up and down with his docket in his hand.

'This is a load of shite, lads,' he says as he throws the docket at the feet of the selectors and heads for the dressing-room. 'You're taking the piss out of me. You won't be seeing me again, I can tell ya that ... Fucking joke of a management.'

He then has an internal rant to himself. 'Don't mind them, Danny. They haven't a clue. You know you're better than half that team. You're not coming back. That's you done.'

He's in far too much of a huff to warm down with the rest of the team. He doesn't even bother showering—just grabs his gear bag and gets into his car and heads home.

This is a regular occurrence, though, and, as sure as day will turn to night, the Danny fella will be first down to training the following Tuesday night, full of energy, in great form and raring to go.

'Well, lads, grand evening for training.'

'Sure is, Danny. Will ya give me a hand setting up this drill?'

'No bother.'

These lads are legends, in my eyes!

The goalkeeper

If I was to sum up every goalkeeper playing the game in one word, that word would be 'nuts'. These head-the-balls are in a league of their own.

For Jaysus' sake, lads!

Ahhhhh Sh#ite!

THE
GOALKEEPER

Have you ever looked into the mad eyes of a stray dog? Well, that's the eyes of a goalkeeper when he's after letting in a howler. A big racking Garryowen has been kicked in from midfield; the goalie shouts, '*Keeper's ball!*' and lets it drop straight through his hands and into the back of the net. Now, instead of turning round and saying to himself, 'Bollocks! I should have caught that'— which the eejit should have—he turns round like a shopkeeper after a load of young lads have trampled his flowers out the front. He lets out an unnatural roar at the wing-back for not tracking his man. 'Billy! Will ya track that number 12, for Jaysus' sake. You're useless.'

In the midst of this madness he'll put the next ball down on his tee, try the 'spectacular' kick-out and nine times out of ten he'll land the ball over the sideline, knocking over the water bottles. I'll tell you something, you're a brave man if you roar into him after that, 'Come on ta fuck, Mackey. Get your head in the game ...'

This is by far the worst thing you can do, because this is when they are at the height of madness and liable to let in another five goals or get sent off.

I once played with a fella who was just after making one of the greatest saves I've ever witnessed. And what does he do only get up, pumped with adrenaline, grab the ball off the ground, fist-pass it straight to the opposition full-forward out of sheer panic and ... *Goal!* He went on to let in another two before half time, and he got sent off on a second yellow with five minutes to go.

Where else would you get someone standing in a field on a horrible day, roaring and shouting like a headbanger, with the ball nowhere near his goal? 'Davey, track back. Mickey, watch the gap. Tom, move ... Move! ... Fucking *move*, Tom!'

The ball would be sailing straight over the black spot, yet they still feel the need to roar:

'Post ...

Post! ... *Possst!*'

When they do make a good save it's like a shot of adrenaline straight to the vein: they leap around the goalmouth, fist-pumping, shouting and roaring.

Hurling goalkeepers are some article—hard to believe that not too long ago you didn't have to wear helmets in the game. Imagine standing in goals for a penalty: a man fourteen yards out is going to hit a sliotar at you as hard as he can, and you with no shield to protect your face. Complete madness!

A rare auld breath is the goalkeeper. They can also be spotted, during a one-sided game, leaning against one of their posts and having a good chat with the umpires.

'Are ye missing many?' asks the umpire.

'Yeah, we're missing a few lads with the county minors and under-21s.'

'Who's that number 10 ye have there? He's fierce handy.'

'Ah, he's class, all right. But the bollox won't train. Loves the pints too much. Can't rely on him at all.'

'Plenty of them boys around, all right ...'

I often wondered why people become goalkeepers. Is it a desire, or what? I'd say 99 per cent of young lads hate playing in goals when they're underage; it was usually the 'less talented' players who were handed the number 1. Or chaps who had a long kick or a solid puck-out. I wonder, though, are you going to tell me that Dublin's Stephen Cluxton, Wexford's Mags D'Arcy or Cork's Anthony Nash aren't talented!

The gym head

This lad is in serious shape, 24/7. A real gym junkie. He has enjoyed playing GAA over the years only because so much is concentrated on 'strength and conditioning'. One of the happiest moments of his life was when the 'tight fit' jersey was brought in; he's the one who's always bringing up the question of clothing at the meetings at the beginning of the year.

THE
GYM HEAD

'I think we should get matching warm-up tops, the tight-fit ones, and skinny tracksuit bottoms. It's important to look well. I want a size small in T-shirts and polo tops ... '

He'll generally wait until all the team have left the dressing-room before waltzing out, dropping shapes left, right and centre as he jogs up for the team photo. He wants all the supporters up on the bank or behind the fence to comment on his physique.

'Jaysus, Nialler is in some shape—massive big arms on him.'

You can often spot them in team photos, puffing the chest out as much as they can in order to look stocky. They might even be on tiptoe if they're standing at the back.

This fella, though, is generally brutal in his ball skills: he's fit as a fiddle but can barely hold a hurl or solo a ball. A great man to lead a 'bleep test' for fitness, though. He's an animal in the gym, and ninety seconds after the warm-down he'll have a protein shake and two of the new protein bars in his gob, talking shite about going to the gym the next day.

'Yeah, I did the chest and arms yesterday, so I'll do the shoulders and forearms tomorrow,' he says, as he peels off the jersey and tenses the six-pack before strolling to the showers, thinking he's a lion strutting about in the jungle.

A lot of GAA players around the country are playing at a fairly decent level thanks to sheer fitness.

The more 'talented' players, well, you don't see as much of them on the ball, because of these 'fit hoors' being up and down the field.

At the top level of inter-county the players are both fitness freaks *and* naturally gifted—near close to robots, at this stage. Scary!

The lad who's always injured

Where do you start with this fella? If it's not the hamstring it's the lower back; if it's not the groin it's the ankle. This man is a pest, spending three-quarters of his season on the treatment table yapping away to the physio about the latest series on Netflix.

THE LAD
WHO'S ALWAYS INJURED

'Have ya seen *House of Cards*?'

'I haven't, no—just in the middle of *13 Reasons Why*.'

'Jaysus, I watched two episodes of that and it was enough for me. Too intense for my liking!'

'Yeah, it's a bit full-on, all right ...'

Whenever he does play a match he might get a good run for a game or two, but then his man might score three or four points off him, and then the old reliable groin gets tight again, the hand goes up, he signals to the line, and off limps Jimmy.

'Well, Jimmy, you okay?'

'Ah, yeah, just strained my right groin a bit. Should be okay for championship.'

This man and the club secretary don't get on too well. At AGMs, when they're stressing over how much money is going towards the physio, most of the attendance have Jimmy on their mind.

'Well, if Jimmy just gave up we'd be in a much better place. The chap is always injured!'

For such players it's most certainly all in their heads. Of course everyone gets injured—that's part and parcel of sport—but there's a big difference between this and doing the dreaded cruciate ligament. (Which, by the way, is becoming far too common among GAA players. Such a pox of an injury: you turn awkwardly and *snap*! Your year is over, and you have a nightmare ahead of going to the gym and doing all your rehab. That's a proper injury.) But these fellas with their 'tweaked hamstrings' and their sore big toe—I'd question them guys, and every club has plenty of them at every level. Cowboys, Ted!

The big, moany full-forward

How many times have you seen this fella in a full-forward line? It's generally for the third team; he's playing probably twenty years and just won't retire. He loves coming down and pissing about and moaning about everything and everyone. From the minute he arrives for any match, he's giving out.

THE BIG MOANY
FULL-FORWARD

'Have we not got the good, big set of jerseys? Don't be handing me them tight-fit ones: they should be left with the under-16s!' 'Will the physio be here tonight to strap up my ankles?' 'These footballs are never pumped!' 'Jaysus, my legs are hanging. Training last Thursday was a killer. I thought he did a bit much, with this game on today.'

He'll moan during the warm-up that his legs are a bit heavy, and he'll spend most of it lying on his arse doing stretches.

Once the ball is thrown in, the roaring and shouting starts—he'll be roaring all sorts out on the field.

'Will ye kick the ball in long?' The ball will be kicked in long, and it will be broke away from him by the full-back.

'Fuck's sake, lads, will ye kick the ball in low to me,' he says, as he asks the keeper for a sup of his water.

Next ball will be kicked in perfectly in front of him, and the full-back will get a fist in and knock it away, and the moany full-forward will end up on his hole. As he drags himself off the ground with embarrassment he'll roar abuse at the ref. 'Ref, ref, push in the fucking back, ref! Are ya blind!'

The ref will ignore him, so he turns to one of the umpires. 'Umpire, you seen that. Do your job, will ya!'

Every team has the 'young lad' who's an up-and-coming star. These big, moany auld full-forwards hate them. It's sheer envy of the potential these nippers may just have to play senior inter-county, which is something the big hatchet-man had always dreamt of doing; but the closest he ever got to it was being brought to an under-14 trial to make up the numbers. So if the young lad does anything remotely wrong in the game, the full-forward will let him know. 'Lay it off, will ya? You're not playing under-16 now.'

At one stage the centre-forward will win a free from the ref, and he'll make a big fuss of it. 'About time, ref. He's been doing that all game.' He'll tell the young lad to 'go on away': he has his free. He'll steady himself as his breathing settles, and then he'll slice the ball miles wide. He'll look at his boot to wonder why it happened, then jog back into position, turn around and roar out to the field for the lads, 'Keep feeding me with the ball!'

I would describe this big lump as:

- carrying a fair few pounds;
- wearing new boots;
- wearing odd gloves or big goalkeeper's gloves;
- wearing well-worn shorts;
- having a huge arse;
- wearing a knee bandage.

He feels that he's always had the ability to play county but that he never got his chance. I think we all know why he didn't get it. I'll say no more!

The characters at every match

The sneery auld lad

Every GAA club has all types of characters, but I think this man takes the biscuit. He prides himself on slagging and abusing everyone at the match,

Ahhh … He's not county shtandard! I'd have scored that myself!

THE SNEERY AULD LAD

whether it's the ref, the umpire, the corner-forward, the linesman—all the way to the person who sells the tea at half time. 'Two euros for a teabag and a drop of hot water! Youse are some shower, d'ya know that!'

An all-round thick auld bollox!

By God, he's never a happy man: a player could score fourteen points in a five-star, outstanding display, but Auld Eugene still wouldn't be happy.

Fellow-supporter: Well, Eugene, Jaysus, that was some win.

Eugene: Ah, we did our best to throw it away.

Fellow-supporter: My God, Tommy was unreal, wasn't he? Fourteen points—some tally. The county manager won't be able to ignore that kind of performance. There aren't much better forwards in the county—not that I've seen, anyway!

Eugene: Ah, he was okay. He's not county standard—no chance. Did you not see the free he missed near the end? I'd have scored that myself!

No matter how good a young talent you are, in his eyes you're either 'too big and too slow' or 'too small and too weak'. There's no pleasing these men whatsoever. You can spot them a mile away at every GAA match, standing there with a sneery head on them—the flat cap, the anorak and the cold, fearful eyes. They won't always tell you to your face that you've had a bad game—they might even tell you that you played well—but the minute you walk away they'll slate you, left, right and centre.

Eugene: Good game, Rory. Fair play ...

Rory: Ah, it was okay, Eugene—tough out there.

Eugene: Ah, no, you played well.

Then you walk round the corner, and Eugene turns to the man beside him.

Eugene: Jaysus, it's worse that chap is getting. Said it for years: he's useless.

Fellow-supporter: Bit harsh there, Eugene. He tries hard.

Eugene: Ah, don't be so soft. He's as much a hurler as I am a pilot!

*

I've heard some classics out of some of these men over the years, on the sideline at both training and matches. 'Here, big fella, big fella: ya may retire. You're useless.' That was shouted at me after playing a poor game for my club *under-16s*!

'Take off that number 5 there and send him to the bog—about as much use for him.'

I was watching a game recently enough, and this man I was standing beside would be old-school, very witty, and he can't stand all the hand-passing that's got into football nowadays. (He prefers the old-style catch and kick—sure who doesn't!) Both teams were playing defensive—it was fairly brutal to watch—and I could see the man getting thicker and thicker: no matter where on the field the ball was, he was roaring, 'Will ya kick the ball in! Will ya kick the ball in!'

With about ten minutes left in the match, he turned round to me and says, 'I'm off, Rory.'

'Where are ya going? There's ten left.'

'I'm going. I can't watch that crap any more. I'd rather be at home washing a dirty lasagne dish with a toothpick than watch any more of that godforsaken handball ... Pure shite!' And he walked over to his car!

The older you get, though, the more you appreciate these characters. When you're a young lad they aren't great to listen to, but the older you get the more you warm to them and understand that they're just die-hard club men who love a good moan about the present crop of club players.

In fairness, they make the GAA what it is. Every club has at least one. In my opinion they're needed to keep these up-and-coming fellas who fancy themselves on their toes.

The crazy, overprotective mother

The GAA really brings the inner madness out of so many people. The passion and excitement of games can sometimes seem to completely change a person's character during the sixty or seventy minutes—and nobody more so than the over-enthusiastic mother on the sideline!

I don't know what it is, but as a young player you can often be at home the morning of a big game, the mother making the breakfast, nice and calm, chatting tactics—the lot. And then ...

> Ah here, No.4, ya dirty bastard! Touch my son again and I'll come over this fence!

THE CRAZY OVERPROTECTIVE
MOTHER

Son: Mam, will you do me a favour and don't lose the head on the sideline today? I could hear you very clear last match shouting at the ref. It's kind of embarrassing, to be honest. I'm sixteen now. I don't need you to get my back. I'm grand.

Mother: Ah, don't be silly. I'm well controlled on the sideline. I love going to watch you play.

Son: Yeah, I know you do, but sometimes you get a bit too excited. So just try not to!

Mother: Don't worry. I won't.

Fast forward to the match: young Peter gets an off-the-ball slap from his marker. Nobody can prepare you for the language that comes out of the overprotective mother's mouth.

Mother: Ah, here! Ah, number 4, ya dirty bastard! Touch my son again and I'll come over this fence and swing for ya ...

The elder son might then turn round to try and control his aggressive mother.

Elder son: Ma, will ya calm down? You're making a show of yourself.

Mother: Ah, I don't give a shit. That dirty fecker over there [pointing her finger at a confused-looking fifteen-year-old] hit my son. Yeah, *you*!

She eventually does calm down, but by then the damage has been done: the fire in the belly has been released!

The gas thing about these wild ladies is that, before and after the ref blows his whistle, they're the most lovely, gentle people you can meet. But once the ball is thrown in, the passion begins to flow, and you better steer clear.

So be warned: when you're next at a GAA match and a woman next to you says, 'That's my son playing out there, wing-forward ... He's a great lad,' I wouldn't be taking any chances if I were you. I'd say, 'Ah, that's very good,' and I'd head off and get a view of the game from the far sidelines! Now, of course, players' mothers aren't all wild, but you'll find a couple at every club game all over the country who ... well, let's just say that they get caught up in the heat of any game their son is involved in!

The knowledgeable Noddy

Whenever there's a GAA quiz, this is your man. This fella goes to every game, the length and breadth of the country. He's not one to sit there abusing refs or players: he just sits and observes—a real fanatic of the GAA.

Mickey is still out with the ankle! He'll probably be out another two games

THE
KNOWLEDGEABLE NODDY

Generally, he's a very quiet, soft-spoken man; he usually has a Club Lemon after matches, and he could be there for hours chatting all things GAA. He knows—I don't know how—absolutely every player, team and manager, in all aspects of any game. If you ever miss a match, Noddy is your man to chat to.

'Good man, Noddy. How's the form?'

'Good, yeah.'

'Were you at the game?'

'I was, yeah.'

'Was Mickey playing, or is he still injured?'

'No, Mickey's still out with the ankle. He'll probably miss another two games. Mark played centre-forward instead. Did well: touched the ball twenty-four times, ran seven kilometres, kicked with his right fourteen times and his left six times, scored three points (one from a 45), hit four wides and gave away the ball three times.'

This man will be spotted at 99 per cent of club matches and will pop the head up at most training matches, standing there observing every player's movement and form.

He might even be taking notes on who's at training, so that in the discussion after the match he'll be able to confirm who has and who hasn't been training in the previous few weeks.

'No, wait, hold on a minute. You can't say he's lost the hunger. Paul hasn't missed a training session this year; he's just going through a bad spell of form. But you can't argue over his commitment.'

Not only can this fella name every winner of the all-Ireland in both hurling and football in the past fifty years but he can also tell you if it was raining, snowing or sunny on them September days. He could tell you who started and what they scored, and how many yellow and red cards were given; he could probably even tell you what the ref, linesmen and umpires had with their tea at half time. ('There's some Jaffa Cakes and Fig Rolls, lads. Work away.')

He lives and breathes the sport; his weekends are dedicated to travelling everywhere to support both club and county. Whether it's an O'Byrne Cup match in January or a club friendly in June, he'll be there watching every ball kicked and sliotar pucked. These men know all things GAA!

The lad who could have played county

Everyone who has played GAA has at one stage wanted to play county— not that many get to. It's arguably the biggest honour in the game to play for your county in a championship match. Every club has the man who reckons he 'could have' played county!

Lad, I'm making a comeback! I was some underage player! Unmarkable!

THE LAD WHO COULD HAVE
PLAYED COUNTY

This fella would be in his forties; he finished playing when he was about nineteen, claiming it was because of bad ankles, but everyone knows it was because he enjoyed the cream of a pint more than the 9 a.m. training sessions. After every game he'd waffle and waffle about how good a minor he was: if he wasn't plagued with the bad ankles he would have been an All-Star.

'I'm telling ye, men, nobody could strike a free like I could. Do ye remember that under-16 game back in 1992? I was unmarkable that day: no matter who they put on me I roasted them—unstoppable. I was some underage player'—as he orders another pint of stout.

For the past fifteen years, whenever he'd have a gallon of drink in him at 2 a.m. in the pub, he'd promise that he'd be making a comeback.

'I'm fucking telling ya here and now, John: I'll be down training next Tuesday evening, and I'll strap up the ankles and see how they go, because I know, myself, if I can get fit I'll guide us to win the championship ...'

'Ah, will ya quiet down, Cian. Sure you're saying that this past ten years.'

'Listen to me: I'll be there. Everyone knows I'm the best player this club has ever had ... '

Of course, for fifteen years and counting, there's been barely any sign of him near training on that

Tuesday. He might pop down once in a blue moon, realise halfway through the warm-up that he's beyond unfit and call it a day ... Again!

If you're at a match in the future and some fella beside you smoking a fag starts telling you about his minor days, and about how good he was, well, you're talking to this fella. Have a bit of craic with him and let on that you remember him, all right, and that he was some player. Bejaysus, he'll have some ammo then for the next year or so!

The fair-weather Dublin supporter

The Dubs bring a spark to the summer, to be fair, whenever they travel outside Croke Park—which isn't too often! They bring the banter to whatever town they're in, as well as the singing and the slagging. There are a lot of true Dublin fans, of course, but there are also plenty of so-called supporters who only enjoy a good day out during the summer.

Come on you boys in blue, come on you boys in blue!

THE FAIR-WEATHER
DUBLIN SUPPORTER

These are some boyos: they can always be seen walking down Clonliffe Road in Dublin in mid-July or early August, when the championship is coming to the latter stages. There's a very slim chance—actually, there's *no* chance—that these lads will be spotted in or around the crowds of O'Connor Park in Tullamore for an O'Byrne Cup match in early January. In reality, these lads are massive Man United, Liverpool, Arsenal or sometimes even Leeds United fanatics; but once the English soccer is done and dusted for the year, they search for excuses to go on 'da gargle', and what better way than a day out in Croke Park.

You'll often hear them before you see them. They'll be sporting a brand-new Dublin jersey, the price tag probably still on half of them, tucked down the back of the neck. They'll have a nice baseball cap on, the peak pointed towards the summer sky, and a can of Dutch Gold or warm cider in their hand, and they'll be chanting, '*Come on*, you ... boys in blue ... *Come on*, you ... boys in blue,' as they storm by the Hogan Stand entrance, shouting and heading for the famous Hill 16.

I created a character for my sketches based on this type of man. I've named him 'Whacker Murphy'—a right motormouth who knows nothing about GAA and just loves following the pints of lager.

Nowadays the bandwagon boyos are more common than ever, for one reason and one reason only: the Dubs are flying high, arguably higher than any other group of players in the team's history. We're witnessing one of the best teams the GAA has ever seen. What's great about this crop of players— and, trust me, the words aren't too easy to muster up, me being a true Meath man—is that they play football the way it should be played: attacking and free-flowing, and all-round great to watch.

They have a group that comes round once in a blue moon. The amazing (and sad) thing about how powerful the Dublin team is at present is that Jim Gavin could leave his best fifteen on the bench till August and he'd probably still win each and every game in Leinster. A scary thought.

You'd have to be happy for the die-hard Dublin fans who made the trips around the country during the tough years, 1996 to 2010, in pursuit of the Sam Maguire. Them I am happy for, but the Whacker Murphys of this world are really milking this team's success, enjoying many a sunny day up on Hill 16, yelling and shouting. If you were to wander up there on a championship day you'd be guaranteed to hear a few things like this:

'Bring on Whelo, for Jaysus' sake ...'

'Number 4, you're bleedin' muck!'

'Give the ball to Brogan! Give it to Brogan!'

'Why is the ref blowin' up for half time? Sure there's ten minutes left, the dozy bollox.' [Someone will inform him that football matches are in fact thirty-five minutes a half, unlike soccer, which is forty-five minutes.] 'Oh, there's only thirty-five minutes a half in the GAA, is there? ... Jaysus, huh!'

'Dermo! Dermo! Dermo! Dermo! ...'

'Here, boys, this is bleedin' muck. 'Mon we head back to my gaff and get the second half of the United game.'

They're some boyos, all right, but it wouldn't be a GAA summer without these fellas drinking cans and singing on the banks of Whitworth Road!

GAA referees

I've always wondered why anyone would want to be a referee—nothing but abuse being thrown at you. There are two types of referee in the GAA: the standard club ref and the over-the-top inter-county ref (or want-to-be inter-county ref).

The club referee

This man has been reffing matches a long time; he knows every player in the county by their first name.

'Mark, calm down now. I don't want to have to book you.'

'Ah, Mick, I barely touched him.'

'Just calm down, Mark ...'

He's the type of man who arrives at the game five minutes before throw-in, getting the boots on while sitting on the edge of the boot of his car.

'Powerful evening for a game, lads—mighty.'

He'll then jog up to the middle of the field and blow his whistle for the captains to come in for the standard pre-match speech.

'Right, men, I don't want to have to use any cards here today, but I won't tolerate any abuse towards me. I had to work today like the rest of ye, so any nonsense or back-chat and I'll be bringing the free forward ten yards every time. Now, heads or tails?'

He'll spend most of the sixty minutes jogging between the two 50s, with the hand up over his forehead when the ball is in either the full-forward line or the full-back line: a chap could get opened up with a box in the square. When this happens, the ref will blow his whistle for calm and jog down to the fourteen-yard line with the whistle in his gob. By the time he arrives at the scene he's too out of breath to decide who hit whom, or to take names, so he calls for a bit of calm and just hops the ball up or throws in the sliotar.

'Cut out the nonsense, fellas. Now play away, men, play away.'

There's a referee in Co. Meath named Mick Ryan—as well known in Meath as Seán Boylan—the definition of 'play on, play on'. Rumour has it that Mick doesn't even bother bringing cards with him to a match. He barely uses the whistle and loves a good free-flowing match. Sure don't we all!

For refs, no matter how a game goes, in the best case they'll have one team coming up after the game wanting to shake their hand. 'Well played, ref, well played.' The ref will then walk ten yards and have the opposing manager in his ear giving out about every decision he gave against his team. Not to mention the abuse shouted at him from the 'hurlers on the ditch' at every match.

'Ah, put on a blue jersey, referee ...'

'Are ya blind, referee! Are ya blind!'

'Where's your whistle, referee!'

'Blow it up ta fuck, referee, blow it up ... '

'Where's your cards, ref, where's your cards!'

'Ref ... ref ... *refff*!'

*

I heard a classic at an under-16s match a few years ago. I was doing the line, and the ref, who was from the home club, was getting a fair bit of stick from an auld lad on the sideline. As the game went on, the ref gave everything in their direction, but with about ten minutes to go he gave a brutal decision against the home team, and the auld lad behind the fence shouts, 'Ah, for Jaysus' sake, ref. Will ya do your job!'

Without even blinking, the ref turns round and shouts back at him, 'My job is to roof houses, and I'm very good at it, so keep your thoughts to yourself.' And he carried on with the game.

The whole sideline burst out laughing. That put a sock in your man's mouth: wasn't a word out of him for the last ten minutes. Brilliant.

I suppose club refs know well what they're signing up for, and they must get a kick out of it. But I can definitely think of a more enjoyable way to spend an hour exercising, that's for sure!

The inter-county referee

Now, this man fancies himself; the modern inter-county ref has to be seen and heard. He'll be as fit as a fiddle —no beer belly on these fellas, so that they don't miss a single thing on the field. He'll be wired up from ear to toe with state-of-the-art equipment so that he'll be able to hold conversations with his linesmen and umpires throughout the match.

THE INTER-COUNTY
REFEREE

'Well, men, this game is flowing nicely here. Keep an eye out for a tug of a jersey: I'm in the humour for dishing out two meaningless yellow cards so I can put some sort of a stamp on this game.'

The black card

Referees have their best games on the big stage, where you don't even notice them on the field. But as if it wasn't already hard enough for refs to avoid abuse, this stupid 'black card'—enforcing substitutions for players who make cynical fouls—comes into play. Fair enough if it's there to prevent a deliberate drag-down in front of goals, but refs using it for misjudged tackles is becoming a joke. Everyone loves a good shoulder in the game, but this rule limits the 'hard-hitting'. If you're a split-second late with your shoulder, and you hit a man a jostle after he releases the ball, it's bye-bye, and you're off to an early shower.

I played a match there two years ago; I was only back after being a year out of football, so I was fairly eager. Within forty-five seconds of the ball being thrown in, their man was running at me. It was Séamus Kenny of Simonstown—a great footballer and servant to Meath. 'Sham' came up along the endline, and I thought this was a perfect chance to lay down a bit of a marker, so I went to put him on his arse. But when I was already committed to the shoulder, didn't the cute little hoor lay off the ball, and *bang!* I caught him straight, full-frontal, in the chest.

The ref jogged over. A black card never even entered my mind: I presumed it was a standard yellow. I thought the black card was only really used above in Croke Park, but out the ref came with the black. 'G'luck, Rory.' After forty-five seconds of a game in early January I was heading for the dugout. 'Complete bollox of a rule,' I says to the ref as I walked off the pitch.

The way players are looking at the new rule, it's not worth trying to land the perfect shoulder, which certainly takes away from the physical side of things in the game we once loved and enjoyed. How many auld lads have you met who complain about how soft GAA has gone nowadays?

'Ah, it's getting to be like the soccer. Fellas aren't allowed touch each other on the field now without the ref booking them. Sure where's the enjoyment in watching that!'

Look at the physicality that's alive and well in hurling: players are still able to get stuck in to each other and aren't worried about throwing their body into a tackle. The black card certainly makes it a tougher job for the poor old refs. I honestly hope it's scrapped in the near future, as it causes nothing but controversy, from where I'm standing.

So, to all the 'men in black' out there: leave the black cards in your pocket or on the kitchen table before you leave the house, fellas. That would be my own advice, and no doubt half the country's!

Doing umpire or the line at club matches

Solid GAA folk love nothing more than heading down to their local pitch to watch a match—a chance to get some fresh air, watch a game and enjoy the banter on the sideline. Most people do get to do this, but at every one of these club matches there's always one person who gets shafted into doing umpire or linesman.

Every club has that fella who loves doing either of these jobs—a great man for giving a dodgy decision in favour of the home side. He'll happily wave a decision towards the home team and get endless abuse from the opposition players and supporters. I think these fellas enjoy that craic.

The same men will be leaning against the post doing umpire, talking all sorts of shite to the goalkeeper.

'Well, are ye missing many?'

'Who's that young lad playing there? Number 12. Jaysus, he's handy.'

'Were ya at the county game last Sunday? Thought the ref rode us, so he did.'

'They'll be doing well to finish this game: it's getting fairly dark.'

'Grand evening for a match, isn't it?'

'Would youse have many on the county panels?'

'Will Kilkenny win the hurling, you reckon?'

'Any chance of a sup of your water, there? 'Tis a shocking warm evening ...'

Not everyone enjoys doing these thankless jobs as much as that fella, though. I think everyone has got stung at least once into doing the line or umpire at a club match.

You decide, last minute, to go watch the game. You're happy sitting out in the car with the lads, having the bit of craic and listening to music before the game starts. Then, out of nowhere, up walks the club chairman and knocks on the window.

'Here, men, we're badly stuck for the line. Will one of ye do it for us?' All of you will put the head down into the phone and say nothing.

'Ah, come on, lads. We just need one of ye.' Then, despite your best efforts, he'll make eye contact with you. 'Right, out you get, young O'Connor ...'

And before you know it you're standing on the line, holding a white flag in the pissing rain, absolutely ragging with yourself that you decided to come to the match in the first place, and all the lads in the car beeping at your every move.

'G'wan, umpire, ya bollox ya.'

'Umpire, umpire, do your job, umpire!'

Of course it'll be one of those games where all the action is on your side, and you get dog's abuse for the sixty minutes—and probably end up with pneumonia from standing in the rain for over an hour, with your soaked socks and runners, and zero thanks at the end of the match for your trouble. If you're very lucky you might get a cup of tea.

But sure that's what the GAA is all about. 'It's not what your club can do for you, but ...' Try telling that to someone doing line on a rainy, windy night in the winter.

The Sunday Game

This programme has been the main source of coverage for the GAA for a long, long time. The majority of Irish people feel that the 'Sunday Game' tune is the sound of the summer—I know I do. Every time I hear the '*do, do, dodiletildoo ... da do da do do do dooo, da da da da do do dooo ...*' it sends a shiver down my spine. The good auld Michael Lyster opens every show with 'Hello, everyone. You're very welcome to *The Sunday Game*.'

Every summer there's always some great debates and conversations on the programme. Over the years it has provided some classic TV moments. Here are some of my favourites.

Pat Spillane's in-depth analysis of the Meath v. Mayo row in 1996

This Mayo–Meath brawl is up there with the biggest on-field rows in GAA history, and Pat Spillane did it justice with this classic commentary. An utter classic analysis from the great Kerryman.

*

Here comes the first blow, where Dempsey hits Darren Fay. Anthony Finnerty comes in just to finish him off a little bit and gives him a touch of the elbow ...

Colm Coyle in the background hitting Finnerty: this is Colm's first punch. Finnerty—delayed reaction—looks around, sees Martin O'Connell coming and thinks that the best action is to go down ...

Here Liam McHale arrives, jumps in, and a wonderful gap opens up. He hits no one at all and goes straight through [laughs]. But unfortunately the entire county of Meath seem to come on top of him, and the poor man got an awful killing in this incident ...

The umpire came out at this stage, but in his wisdom he removed himself again ...

And here in this incident watch Jimmy McGuinness, number 8. He arrives on the scene; he exercises his right leg a little bit here—stretching, I presume. Continues on then, and he meets Colm McMenamin. Watch him there: he's looking for a little bit of action. He looks around; he just tries to trip some fella—runs along, and who does he meet but the unfortunate Colm McMenamin. He does a nice little bit of sumo-wrestling impersonation here. Fair play to McMenamin: he held his ground, and McGuinness couldn't drop him.

Joe Brolly's rant about Seán Cavanagh

By Jaysus, this was some rant. I remember it very well. With Joe you just know by the head on him that when the camera turns to the panel for their opinion he's waiting to let loose. And after Seán Cavanagh of Tyrone dragged Conor McManus down to make sure he wasn't going to get a last-minute goal in the 2013 all-Ireland quarter-final, you could see that Brolly was ready to hit the roof, saying that 'you can forget about Seán Cavanagh, as far as he's a man ...'

It was great TV, to be fair. My favourite part was when he says, 'Nobody has stood up for Tyrone during the 2000s more than I have in this studio, when they were getting all sorts of abuse from you and from you,' as he aggressively points his finger at a shocked Pat Spillane and Colm O'Rourke. These rants are always great TV to watch.

Joe Brolly and Pat Spillane on Colm Cooper

Another one of my favourites is when Joe Brolly and Pat Spillane were discussing the talent and career of Colm 'the Gooch' Cooper. Joe was adamant that the Gooch isn't one of the greats (which of course he is), with the bulling head on Pat beside him, disgusted with what Joe had to say about one of Kerry's greatest footballers.

'Joe, Joe ...'

Joe ignores him, of course—an impossible man for letting you get a word in when he's in flow—and he continues on.

Pat keeps nodding the head. He looks up at Michael Lyster. 'He's digging, Michael. He's digging.'

*

There is one thing you'd have to say about Joe Brolly: he's a very tough man to win an argument against. His sheer intelligence and his incredible memory make any arguing with him very tough. Even if he's talking pure shite, his way with words makes you think he has everything sussed. I for one enjoy his banter on the programme. Whether he's doing it out of pure passion or for attention—who knows. But he certainly adds to the programme, that's for sure.

An honest answer

On *The Sunday Game*, and on TV in general, the difference between what you're thinking and what you actually say is a big factor. If you were to listen to any of the pundits in a clubhouse on an 'Up for the

Match', you'd get a lot more banter out of them than you would on RTÉ of a Sunday night. Each person on *The Sunday Game* panel brings to it their own individual character.

If everyone spoke with brutal honesty we would have very entertaining TV. Below is an example of what we would be in for if this were the case.

*

Michael Lyster: The panel for today's all-Ireland final between Dublin and Kerry are the ever-present Colm O'Rourke, Pat Spillane and Joe Brolly. Well, men, you're all very welcome here today. What are your predictions for what should be a great game of football?

Colm: To be honest, Michael, I don't give a shite who wins. It's hard to figure out who I want to win less. The Dubs are my greatest rivals, and if they win today I'll have to listen to fuckin' eejits shouting at me on the way to my car this evening. On the other hand, if Kerry win I'll have this parrot Spillane beside me raving about how good Kerry are, and saying that it's all about 'pure football'. So, yeah, I'll sit here and let on I give a shite, but I'm most looking forward to my roast-beef dinner after the game.

Michael: Ah, good man, Colm, you're in mighty form. Joe, what's your thoughts on today's encounter? Now, you have only two or three minutes, Brolly, so please shut up after that!

Joe: Well, Michael, I'm quite frankly praying for some drama here today so that I can open up my lungs and go on a complete rant about a specific event in the game about which I'm going to use words that most people can't even spell, in order to sound like I'm so intelligent that I just couldn't possibly be wrong in any argument. If these two beside me try to argue with my point I'll up the ante by lowering my glasses till they're nearly falling off my nose, and I'll wave my finger at them in the region of ninety miles an hour till they back off.

Michael: Ah, fair play, Joe, you do that. [Turning to Pat] Mr Kerry himself, Pat, I presume you're hoping that the Sam Maguire is heading for the Kingdom this evening.

Pat: I certainly am, Michael, and let me tell you this short story that makes no sense. In

Kerry we kick-pass the ball any chance we get, and we're all comfortable in possession; this comes from learning the basic skills at a very young age. When I was a young chap I used to solo the ball three miles to the shop, kick it into a local farmer's tractor, go into the shop and buy some Kerrygold for the spuds, collect my ball, solo three miles home and kick the ball into my father's shed from seventy-nine yards, and head off in and have the spuds. I'd often forget the milk, so up I'd get to collect the ball, and off I went soloing again, three miles up and three miles back, this time using my left foot. Now, in any man's language that's twelve miles. I would do that up to three times a week, which is ...

Joe [trying to interrupt]: It's, eh, thirt—

Pat: Joe, zip it ... Thirty-six miles is what it is, Michael, and people often ask what kind of dedication it took to win eight all-Ireland medals, and I tell them that story.

Michael: Good man, Pat. I'm sure half the people have tuned out after hearing that pure waffle. But, anyway, who will win today?

Pat: Yerra, my ... my heart says Kerry, but my head says that I shouldn't have drunk that last pint of porter in Jury's last night. I could do with a chicken-fillet roll and a bag of King crisps right now, to sort myself out. Also, who can I complain to about the toilets having no toilet paper in them? Before we came on air I had a very enjoyable shite while reading today's programme, before realising that there was no toilet paper. I panicked for five minutes before having no option but to use one of my good socks. Not a great start to the day, but, listen, if we can win midfield, Kerry by two.

Michael: Ehhh, okay ... I was wondering why you had only the one sock on now. Anyway, moving on ... Joe, what d'you reckon?

Joe: To be honest with you, Michael, after what Pat just said I want nothing to do with this. I did the same as Pat a few years back while [pointing] you, and you, sat there making me feel dreadful about using my sock to clean myself. But because this man has won eight all-Irelands it's brushed under the carpet, and we move on. Nope, not a man.

Michael: Joe, relax. The game hasn't even started and you're already falling out with the panel. Colm, quickly over to you before we head to the action.

Colm: I myself was wondering why Pat had only the one sock on. Good man, Spillane—happens to the best of us. Ah, listen, Michael, I'm just looking for a good game of football so that I can try not to be too boring in my review of the first half. I'll do my best, but, ya see, my dreary Meath accent is tough to excite anyone with, but I'll do my very best.

Michael: Fair play to ya, Colm, that would be great. Okay, folks, join us after the break, when we'll have the throw-in to this year's all-Ireland football final.

*

Now wouldn't that level of honesty be entertaining of a Sunday afternoon? *The Sunday Game*, though, really is the heartbeat of an Irish summer, and long may it continue.

The post-match interview

Post-match interviews in the GAA these days are almost a waste of time: before a player or manager even opens their mouth you have a fair idea of the standard speech they're going to give. Here's two examples, from a player and then a manager interview scenario.

Player

Let's just say this inter-county star is after having the game of his life on the surface of Croke Park. He's after kicking thirteen points, eight from play: he could not have had a better seventy minutes. He's scored from all angles, set up two goals, tracked back, kicked two 45s. Overall, a ten-out-of-ten performance.

After the game he is of course selected as man of the match. Here's what he'll say to the interviewer, versus what he's really thinking.

*

Reporter: Hi, Bernard. Congrats on a great win and an absolute Rolls-Royce performance from yourself. You must be delighted.

Player says: Of course, yeah—really was a tough battle. The lads worked very hard out on the field and made everything very easy for me inside.

Player thinks: Ah, would ya stop—never had a game like that in my life. I really was incredible.

Reporter: Some of the scores you kicked really were from the top drawer. Take a look at this one here: forty-five yards out on the wing, against the breeze, three men around you—and somehow you managed to take your score.

Player says: It was a bit of a shot out of nothing: nine times out of ten that would never come off. I was just very lucky, to be honest.

Player thinks: Have you seen a better point in Croke Park? That's the best point I've ever kicked in my entire life. I knew exactly what I was doing.

Reporter: Well, you are our selection for man of the match. Here's a man from the local bank to present you with your Waterford Crystal. Will you go and celebrate a great win tonight?

Player says: Thank you. Ah, there won't be much celebrating done: we'll get a recovery session in tomorrow and prepare for our next challenge, which will no doubt be a very tough game.

Player thinks: Cheers. Ah, I'll defo have to have few pints after that game—might even venture into Copper's later on—see what the craic is. I'll surely get a woman after that performance.

*

Wouldn't it be refreshing to hear a player speak with pure honesty after a game? He would 100 per cent be more liked for it.

Manager

Managers, of course, don't like to say much after games: 'tis all hush-hush. I know, respect where it's due, and all that, but some interviews are a bit embarrassing.

Here's an example. Take it that the Dubs are after beating a minnow in the first round of the Leinster Championship by 25 points, and their next opponents are another so-called minnow, in Croke Park—a game where the odds will be along the lines of Dubs 1/50, Minnows 25/1.

This is what you'll hear from Jim Gavin, versus what he's thinking.

*

Reporter: Good man, Jim. Thank you for joining us. A very convincing win, to say the least.

Jim says: Yeah, it was a good performance. I thought the opposition played well and made us work hard for long periods. We just managed to pull away in the final quarter.

Jim thinks: Yeah, it was straightforward. Fair play to the minnows, and all that, but it was a bit of a pasting.

Reporter: You move on now to face [another minnow county] in the quarter-final. How will you prepare for the game? It must be tough when you're 1/50 with the bookmakers to pick up the win.

Jim says: We'll prepare just like we would for any other team. I'm sure it will be a good battle—no easy walkovers these days. Each county is putting in a lot of work, so I'm looking forward to two weeks' time and to what I'm sure will be a good game.

Jim thinks: Ah, listen, these games don't do anyone any good. I'd probably rather have an in-house A v. B game to see how lads are going, but we'll go and no doubt win pulling up and move on to the next game.

*

It'll be a long time before that kind of honesty is heard after matches on the TV, but I'll tell ya something: if ya asked a few characters managing club teams, they wouldn't be long telling you the craic!

Going professional

Will the GAA ever go professional? This is a question that's thrown around a lot these days, especially given how professionally the inter-county teams prepare for championship: no stone left unturned, every last detail looked at to try and get the extra 1 per cent on the field.

Jaysus, personally, I hope it doesn't end up going professional! Isn't that why it is what it is? The joy and pride of wearing your club and county jersey—if the game went professional sure all the morals the GAA stand for would go belly-up.

Mind you, there's certainly a few bob being thrown around in the capital city in order to have an outside county star or two join their ranks. It used to be that if you were a guard or a schoolteacher working in the area you'd be sniffed out and asked to join the local club team, all above board; but in the Dublin scene in the past few years there are without doubt a few brown envelopes being exchanged in order to get the country men on board. This is the kind of thing that's going on:

'Hello?'

'How's it going, Paul? It's the chairman here from [a top-four club in Dublin].'

'Good man. What can I do for you?'

'Listen, I know you've moved up to the area recently, and I'm just enquiring about a potential transfer to ourselves for the year. We have great facilities and a right good young team here that would benefit from your experience.'

'I haven't thought about it, to be honest.'

'Well, sure how does a brown envelope the weight of a bag of sugar sound to you? Under the radar, of course.'

'That doesn't sound too bad to me ...'

'Excellent. We're training tomorrow night at eight. Do you think you can make it?'

'I'll see you there at 7:45. Good luck.'

This of course goes on now, as it has for a number of years. Imagine if the sport did go professional: how much cowboy shite would go on!

*

Here's a conversation that happens in every GAA club when you press an old stalwart on the question of the GAA going professional:

'Well, Jimmy, the GAA has come on some amount since your day. Jesus, I'd say you don't know what to make of it at the minute. Sure it's as good as professional.'

'It certainly has, but not for the better. 'Tis got far too serious now. Referees are ruining the game with all the whistle blows, and don't get me started on that stupid black card. Next thing now they'll bring the black card into hurling, and if they do, that'll be the end of the GAA as we know it—be as bad as soccer to watch then. Fellas will be going round hugging each other on the field. Scandalous carry-on!'

'Would you like to see the sport turn professional, and see the players get paid for their commitment—which, to be fair, is ridiculous at the minute?'

'Professional! Get paid! Are ya out of your mind, young man! It's bad enough nowadays the way it is, fellas walking round thinking they're great, dressed in women's clothes, jeans on their legs that are too small for them, injured half the time, and their heads stuck in mobile phones all day long. Imagine if they had a hefty bank balance as well! Sure they won't even have a chat with someone like myself about the good old days, when GAA players were real men—not like the mollies of today.'

'Ah, I know what you mean. But look at the standard the game is at now: the fitness is unreal. Sure the likes of Brian Mullins or Mick Lyons from your day wouldn't last ten minutes in Croke Park nowadays. They'd be carried off with exhaustion!'

'G'way and don't be annoying me, gossoon. Mullins and Lyons were men on the football field—gave hits and took them as well—they'd put manners on some of the so-called "class acts" these days.'

'Ha, would ya stop now, Jimmy. They wouldn't be able to lay a finger on them, never mind hit them: they'd be skinned alive and have a record number of black cards between them.'

'Well, all I know is it was better to watch back in them days—none of this pussy-footing around with short kick-outs. Makes ya sick ...'

'It's all tactics, Jimmy. Nothing matters more than winning, and managers will do whatever they can to win a game. They don't care about what the likes of myself and yourself think of how they play.'

'Well, if it does go professional before my time is up, I won't be wasting my pension on going to watch it. Pint of stout when you're ready, there, barman.'

A year in the GAA

January

The slog

There's no two ways about it: January is the toughest month of them all on the training front. That first team meeting of the year—the enthusiasm, the preseason hype, the numbers and the great intentions.

The team meeting will be a packed house, to the manager's delight. 'Right, men, we have thirty-five here tonight. This is a great statement of intent.'

There will be no more than nineteen at training come the middle of May, when the evenings get brighter. Same craic every year in every club.

But now each and every man there is eager to give the club, the parish and the community total commitment.

'Lads, this will be our year. If we can give 100 per cent we will win the championship. I have no doubt in my mind'—says the first-team manager with a look of madness in his eyes: he too is full of beans after the winter break.

Before all the running, sweating and slogging comes the fitness test, to see how our bodies are after the over-indulging that comes with Christmas.

You'd be lying at home on the couch with the January blues, struggling not to finish off the last selection box, when the phone buzzes. In comes the dreaded text to the WhatsApp group.

> *Manager:* Well, men, we will be doing the bleep test in the parish hall on Sunday morning, first group at 9 a.m., and second group at 9:30. Names below of who's in which group. See youse then.

Straight away the lads' WhatsApp group goes ninety.

> *Marko:* Bleep test?? Oh Jesus Christ the thoughts of it make me sick.

> *Davey:* [crying emoji].

> *Tony:* Lads, I haven't run since last September [blushing emoji].

> *Mickey:* This is going to be torture, I'll 100 per cent get sick.

> *Barry (OZ):* [LOL emoji] Hahaha. Enjoy, men, I'll be thinking of yiz Sunday when I'm lying on the beach [sunglasses emoji].

*

On the Sunday morning, lads will arrive at the parish hall one by one, each fella with a look of fear written on his face. The manager will put them through a quick warm-up, then call them into a circle.

'Right, lads, I expect all of you to get to at least level 12. That's the minimum.' The fitness freaks on the team relish this test and look forward to getting to a ridiculous level, while the majority of the panel just want to get through it and not be in the bottom three.

Looking around you, you can see each lad left and right of you panting and puffing, every part of your body telling you to stop—a body still full of porter, turkey and selection boxes ...

Beep! Start of level 11.

'Oh Jaysus Christ, another full level to go before I can pull out,' you think, as the legs are getting heavier and heavier. What always happens is that nobody wants to be the first lad out, but once someone throws in the towel, men drop like flies all around.

Beep! Start of level 12.

'For fuck's sake, will one of youse pull out!' says the big, lazy full-forward, who's as white as a ghost and has a smell of Jameson whiskey coming from every pore in his body.

When everyone is finished cheering on the greyhound of the team as he does a couple of levels all by himself, the manager will call everyone back in—water bottles and heavy breathing everywhere—

and no matter how good or bad the results are, the same speech will be given every year.

'Okay, men, decent effort this morning, but we have a lot of heavy training to do before we're anywhere near where we need to be. I'll see youse Tuesday, on pitch for 7:45 p.m. sharp. Drink plenty of water and eat well between now and then.' In other words, *'I'm going to run the absolute shit out of yiz.'*

*

Whatever it is about the slog in January, it's torture. You do runs after push-ups after runs on the dirty bog of a second pitch, the floodlights as powerful as a candle. You can see fuck-all around you but the dirt and the muck—no sign of a football or sliotar—and there's the deafening sound of the manager's whistle blowing for each sprint. 'That's it, men, keep 'er lit—be worth this pain come the championship.'

Your legs are heavy, you can barely breathe with the sharp January air and you're not sure which end of your body the waste is very close to coming out of. You're just all-round bolloxed.

Then you play a couple of in-house training matches to see where lads are, fitness-wise and skill-wise. These games are, to say the very least, extremely ugly on the eye—desperate standard.

A typical game would consist of a massive amount of heavy breathing; terrible decision-making on the ball; a lot of roaring and shouting at each other ('Johnny, Johnny, cover my man, there, will ya?'—because I'm literally too fucked to chase him myself!); very few scores, a lot of wides and balls into keepers' hands; and plenty of 'tight hamstrings' and old injuries surfacing with ten minutes to go.

'You okay there, Paul?' asks the manager.

'Ah, yeah, not too bad—can just feel the back tighten up a bit. Better leave it at that.'

What Paul really means is 'To be honest with ya, Martin, I'm beyond unfit. That young minor is after kicking three points off me already. I am in my hole going to stand in there as full-back and let him tear me a new one! It's easier to just let on that my back is stiff and call it a day.'

This kind of training lasts about three weeks. You'd like to say it gets easier each week, but it simply doesn't.

The sight of the manager finally taking a bag of footballs out of the boot of his car on the last Tuesday of January is a thing of beauty. Everyone is like a spring chicken when the bag of balls is thrown in to the middle of the group and lads get to kick around.

The AGM

Nearly every club's annual meeting takes place in January. You can be certain that most clubs have the same faces at it every year. For some old club members it's like Christmas—a chance to give out about everyone and everything at the club. There are some standard rants you'll hear at every AGM throughout the country.

'Excuse me, Mr Chairman, but I feel that the adult hurlers aren't doing enough for this club off the pitch. Not too many of them lads have sold lotto tickets on a Friday night.'

'The yearly bill from the club physio is shocking expensive: too many lads taking advantage with just a sore thumb!'

'I suggest five euros a week off all players to help pay for the floodlights.'

'Club membership has to be paid by 31 January, otherwise you will *not* be allowed tog out, at any level. We can't take any risks!'

'The dressing-rooms are left in a dreadful state after training of a Tuesday and Thursday night. There should be a sign welded on to the door telling you to take your boots off, or, for Jaysus' sake, at least to kick the muck off them.'

'We need a new set of O'Neill's footballs for the ladies' team. We had to use mainly inter-county balls all last year—very unfair.'

'I suggest we host a "Strictly Come Dancing" this year for a fundraiser. St Michael's did it last year, and a fella I work with said they made a forty-grand profit.'

'We need more structures at underage: too many old-school people are over our underage teams, not enough people with a clue. We're miles behind some clubs and what they're doing at underage. We'll be left behind, with no hope of winning a championship for the next fifty years.'

If you were to ask anyone in any GAA club to name three-quarters of the regular attendance at their AGMs, it wouldn't be a bother to them. To be fair, it's these stalwarts in every club who make the GAA what it is: grass roots!

What it takes to be an inter-county player

Years ago county players would 'winter well' and come back with a big fat arse on them in January, although they'd be in shape come March or April. They can't afford that luxury any more, though, because the standard of inter-county is as close to professional as you can get: nearly every player needs to mind themselves all year round. It's scary the commitment that's now expected from these players—madness when you consider that we're an *amateur* organisation!

Going to insta the f##k out of this meal prep!

WHAT IT TAKES TO BE AN
INTER-COUNTY PLAYER

Here's some of what it takes to play at the inter-county level.

Diet. All clean eating: no crap whatsoever. Even a big feed of spuds is now frowned on—too many heavy carbohydrates. 'What about a Big Daddy XL whopper meal from KFC?' says you. No chance!

Training. Ah, sure, where do ya start? Six to seven days a week. If you're not on the pitch you're in the gym; if you're not in the gym you're in the pool; if you're not in the pool you're in the yoga class. You'd be out of breath just thinking about what these players go through to be ready for the summer.

Technology. Log every gym session you do; log every meal you eat; log if you're feeling happy or sad when you wake up in the morning!

Managers worried about this level of commitment might be heard having a conversation like this:

'Did ya hear Dublin train twice a day? Before work and after work ...'

'Yeah, serious. Well, that's it: we have to train *three* times a day. We'll do a weight session in the morning, we'll get them to log a yoga or spinning class during their lunch break at work or college and we'll do a ball session that evening on the pitch. Then we'll be up to the pace of the Dubs!'

This commitment is all well and good if you're born in Kerry, Dublin, Kilkenny or Tipperary: you'd have a decent chance of being successful, and all the training and commitment would be worthwhile. But what about the minnow counties who train just as hard? And for what? Nothing but abuse after yet another defeat. You'd be out having a few well-earned drinks in your local pub, and up comes this eejit to ya, just banging of cigarettes and vodka and Red Bull.

'My God, how are you an inter-county player! I'd do better myself. That's the worst county team I've ever seen. And why are you even having a pint? You should be home in bed!'

Look at the likes of Bernard Brogan, Colm Cooper, Henry Shefflin and Joe Canning, getting plenty back from what they give to the GAA: sponsored cars, brand deals, you name it. But what about poor Billy from Wicklow, Dessie from Carlow and Marty from Leitrim, breaking their bollox for years, missing out on holidays, stag parties, weddings. Fair? Will it ever change? Hard to see it. I feel it's a case of the rich getting richer and the poor getting ... well, a bit of mileage allowance and a new pair of boots!

February

In February the club scene and National League get under way. It's also a busy month for the college heads, with the Fitzgibbon and Sigerson Cups in full flow. On the club scene the majority of the running and slogging is nearly done, usually the first round of the league is on and everyone is eager: not only to get playing competitive matches again but also to have a few pints after the first match. Some lads will have been strong and will have pulled through 'dry January'.

After training on the Thursday before the first league match, the changing-room would be fairly buzzing.

> 'Ya heading out for a few pints after the match on Sunday, Mark?'

> 'I am indeed. Absolutely dying for a few—haven't had a sup since New Year's.'

Such a stereotypical Irish thing—dry January—so proud of ourselves for staying off the beer for four weeks. Not everyone can last the month though ...

> 'Fancy a pint the weekend?'

> 'Nah, I'm off it for January.'

> 'Fair play to ya. You're dead right.'

> 'Would ya not go off it yourself for a few weeks?'

> 'Ah, I tried, but I only lasted twelve days. Had a cousin's wedding on—was in my hole going to be standing around drinking MiWadi all day. So that was the end of that. Ya know, yourself!'

February is dominated on the inter-county scene by the National League: all teams from divisions 1 to 4 battle it out, getting themselves in line for the coming championship. Each county will have two or three fresh faces in their team, generally lads who had a solid campaign in the Mickey Mouse pre-season comps: the O'Byrne Cup, the McKenna Cup, the Walsh Cup and so on. These new players will be buzzing and champing at the bit to play inter-county.

A few things you'll notice in a club player who's after getting his chance with the county are that he'll have lost weight and toned up and be looking as fit as ever; he'll have new boots; he might not speak to people he once spoke to; he won't be seen drinking a few pints of a Saturday afternoon with the lads any more; and he'll probably find himself a girlfriend over the Christmas and will be spotted in the local cinema every weekend, having a large bottle of water with his nachos.

*

On the hurling front, February is a big month for ordering the new hurls and taping and gripping them; there's an excitement for the drier, warmer 'hurling weather' ahead.

Different players prefer different hurls. An old-school corner-back or full-back never cares too much about their hurl: any auld thing with a bit of tape on it would do the job. They often use the same hurl for training, playing matches and slapping the back arse off a few cattle on the farm—and then back it would go into the boot of the car for training that night.

Now, up the far end of the field it's a different story: the cocky free-taker treats a good hurl like a family member. He has it taped to perfection, and if he breaks it during a game it's like a tragedy.

CRACK!

Free-taker: Ah, for fuck's sake …

Manager: What's wrong, TJ?

Free-taker: Ah, I'm after cracking the shaft of my hurl.

Manager: Lads, lads, throw a hurl in to TJ there …

TJ would be thrown a hurl he doesn't 'feel too comfortable with', and he'd probably use this as an excuse to do absolutely fuck-all for the rest of the game, going around with a puss on him!

'Can't believe I broke my good hurl' will be his thought for the remainder of the game, and when he does strike a free wrong, and it sails off wide, he'll look down at the face of his hurl as if it were to blame.

*

The ball work in hurling is always tough at training during the early months: crappy lights, soft ground and stiff bodies. The 'first touch' would be all over the shop. It's a vital part of the game nowadays—'tis all about the speed of your first touch. You'll often hear managers roaring, 'First touch, first touch!' from the sideline.

The first touch is a lot easier to manage nowadays: thirty years ago, when sliotars got wet on a dirty, rotten day, they carried weight, and the hurls were a lot heavier. You'd know all about it when you got a sliotar to the shin on a wet day—like a bowling ball being shot at you from a cannon. If ever there was a sport more suited to the dry weather, it's hurling.

Sigerson and Fitzgibbon Cups

During February the Sigerson and Fitzgibbon Cups, for college GAA, will be in full flow. There's always a massive amount of talent involved in college GAA. Sure the standard that hurling and football are at these days is as close to professional as you can get.

Each college will be littered with All-Stars, up-and-coming legends of the game and all-Ireland winners. Given the demands placed on inter-county players at the minute, college suits them down to the ground: plenty of time to recover after training and matches. It's a great opportunity to play with and against some of the best talent out there.

The dominant Dublin colleges in the sport— UCD, DCU and DIT—will have players from all over the country: you'd often see a Kerryman, a Dub and a young talent from Carlow on the same team. The same applies to the likes of UCC and NUI Galway. Then, up north, you have the likes of UUJ (at Ulster University), Queen's and St Mary's.

I will have to give a special mention to St Mary's, who this year (2017) won the Sigerson, beating the defending champions, UCD, in the decider. The amazing stat about this is that the college of St Mary's has a total of only 900 pupils, a mere third of these being male. Their win is an incredible achievement: it just goes to show you that, if you get a bunch of committed people together, anything is possible.

A lot of these players who play inter-county as well as college will be hoping to hang on to their college lifestyle for as long as they can. Sure wouldn't you, if a scholarship came your way? You have your college fees paid for, you have free accommodation and you can train as much as you like, without having to worry about dragging yourself out of bed at 7 a.m. to head for a building-site.

There are always egos about at colleges—lads floating around wearing their county tracksuits, wanting to tell everyone that 'I play county'. Your standard college GAA star will have the following as they stroll around campus:

- skinny tracksuit bottoms;

- the county half-zippy, their initials on the shoulder;

- the popular haircut: tight back and sides, with a muff on top;

- clean-as-you-like Adidas jogging runners (more than likely freebies);

- a bulky watch (it doesn't always tell the correct time—more for show!);

their head stuck into their phone 80 per cent of the time, checking Snapchat, Twitter, Instagram and Facebook.

The 'county' college player doesn't let on, but he adores himself. Once you spot a senior inter-county player wearing his county tracksuit around the campus, you know that his profile picture on Facebook is probably of him with the top off, guns out, sunglasses on and drinking a glass of white wine in the south of France. As he walks round the college he'll be saying the following five things to himself each and every day:

- I am a legend;
- she 100 per cent fancies me;
- I am in serious nick;
- I should have a statue of myself put up outside the gym;
- I am by far the best player in this college.

The weekends of the Sigerson and the Fitzgibbon are always great craic, with the semi-finals being played on the Friday, and the finals being played on the Saturday. It's probably the competition with the most competitive action throughout the month of February, and you're always guaranteed a few humdingers of matches.

March

March is a busy month on the GAA front. They say the biggest day in club football is St Patrick's Day, when the all-Ireland club finals, in both hurling and football, take place in Croke Park. It's quite simply every club player's dream to line out with the lads they played with from underage—brothers, cousins and best friends—but, to be fair, it's very few and far between the club player who gets to experience this.

Traditionally a lot of strong clubs with history see Croke Park on St Patrick's Day: Crossmaglen of Co. Armagh, St Vincent's of Co. Dublin and Nemo Rangers of Cork would be strongholds in the football. In hurling, Portumna of Co. Galway, Ballyhale Shamrocks of Co. Kilkenny and Birr of Co. Offaly, to name just a few, have seen great days in Croke Park on 17 March.

*

I've been to a good few all-Ireland club finals myself—great buzz. What always sticks out is the number of tourists from overseas at the matches, over to celebrate St Patrick's Day in the most Irish place possible, Croke Park.

Sitting next to them can be very entertaining, to say the least. Here's some of the stuff that can often be overheard:

'Oh, my God, what a sport! They're fighting with wooden sticks. Incredible!'

'Why are people celebrating when the ball went over the crossbar!'

'It's Ireland, it's St Patrick's Day, yet we're not allowed bring our beers back to our seats. Strange ...'

'I heard in the toilet that, whatever team wins, they'll drink beer for a whole week!

*

To be fair, some of the GAA phrases you hear at matches must be very tough to make sense of if you haven't grown up in a GAA environment. I've broken down a few of the more popular ones so that, when you're at your next GAA match, you'll know what the sayings really mean.

'Ah, for Jaysus' sake, ref, you're riding us.'

Meaning: Referee, will you please do your job and referee this game fairly. You seem to be giving our opponents a lot of easy frees.

'Ah, come on and get stuck in, lads.'

Meaning: The next chance you get I want you to shoulder your man as hard as you can. Or at least push him in the back and follow through with your knee.

'Sure he is as windy.'

Meaning: You are afraid of your own shadow, and if there is even the slightest chance of you getting hurt you will let your opponent win the ball.

'He ran the shite out of us at training.'

Meaning: The manager feels that the players are not up to the required fitness level, and so he made them run more than they usually would during a standard training session.

'Ah, ref, such a wild pull.'

Meaning: One player has swung his hurl very carelessly and has therefore nearly caused some damage to his opponent.

'Steps, ref! Steppps!'

Meaning: The player has carried the ball a distance without playing the ball—a hop or solo or a touch of the sliotar off the face of the hurl. Four steps and you have to take a play.

'There's loads of timber on the line. Don't be afraid to pull hard.'

Meaning: We have many spare hurls in the kit bag, so feel free to break as many as you like. Just as long as you win the ball.

'Take your points, and the goals will come.'

Meaning: Keep putting the ball over the bar until there's five minutes to go and you're seven points down, then go bonkers and go for goal from every angle of the field.

The 'college heads' return

March is the month when the college heads begin to show their faces back at club training. They rock up in their 'Sigerson gear', thinking they're the dog's bollox, a right real swagger to them as they enter the changing-rooms. A typical conversation would be:

Sneery selector: Ah, good man, Jay. Good of you to come down and join us for a training session. How's the body?

Jay: Not too bad—tough few weeks with the college—so I'll be taking it handy enough for a session or two.

Selector: I'd say that, all right: legs tired from standing in the queue at Copper's—about all that's wrong with ya. I was in college myself, many moons ago, so I know well the craic. If ya tell me a good story I'll leave ya be. A married man like myself lives off stories from youse young lads.

Jay [laughing]: I've a girlfriend the past six months, chief, so not much to tell, I'm afraid.

Selector: A girlfriend during your college days! Silly man. You'll regret that when you're my age, stuck watching *Coronation Street* with herself every night, wishing I was a wilder man in college!

*

The month of March on the training field is a bit more enjoyable—lots of lads have lost the Christmas belly and are in good form. There certainly won't be the same number of bodies at training in the middle of March as there was pledging their life to the club in the first week of January—no chance. These lads will have got the Christmas out of the system and might come back training the very odd time.

Training

The club championship is only around the corner, so preparation is in full flow. 'Tis all about *intensity, intensity, intensity* in the lead-up to club championship: mad, wired managers getting very excited at the thought of lads pealing each other with shoulders on the training field. They'll be happy to see some rattiness coming into training the week or two before the championship. An odd scuffle or argument at training never did a team any harm, they'll tell you.

A typical rant in the huddle in the lead-up to championship would be:

> 'Lads, I want a bit of a bite to training tonight. No silly stuff, but I want to see a difference in your attitudes. Championship is coming, and, as ye know, there are plenty of places up for grabs. Nobody is guaranteed a starting jersey!'

This is the greatest load of shite you'll ever hear. The manager has at least twelve or thirteen lads in mind who will 100 per cent start, but, managers being managers, they need to say what players want to hear—keep everyone happy!

It can be tough preparing for the start of club championship, as you're starved of your county players, because of their commitment to the county. Any club team with plenty of talent is always under pressure for the league, as their key men are unavailable. Once they're back from county duty, Billy and Dermot are back on the bench warming their toes!

It can be tough on the club players at times too. To be fair, the county player has some schedule these days, compared with twenty or thirty years ago. Here's what the county player's schedule looked like 'back in the day', in the 1970s, 80s and early 90s:

Monday. Rest from Sunday's match, i.e. watch *Nationwide*!

Tuesday. Quick fifteen-minute chat before training, to discuss the previous weekend's match. 'Lads, it's simple: we just weren't fit enough. We need to up the number of laps we run, to catch up with the big guns.' Then on the pitch for a mixture of running (laps, laps and more laps), backs-and-forwards and shooting.

Wednesday. Rest, and eat plenty of spuds and veg. 'What's a "gym"?'

Thursday. A lighter session (three-quarters the number of laps from Tuesday), backs-and-forwards, followed by some tactics, e.g. 'Kick every second ball in on top of Bomber. The two corner-forwards scrap for breaks. Everyone understand?'

Friday. During the summer, head down to the field to kick a few points, followed by five or six pints of plain in the local.

Saturday. During the champ season, today would be dedicated to a short and light kick-around. And a brief meeting afterwards to discuss the tactics for Sunday's match.

Sunday. Match day. Meet at the venue thirty minutes before the game. The bus arranged for championship matches at £1 per head. Pre-match tactics discussed two minutes before throw-in. 'Go out there, lads, and give her 100 per cent. *Die* for the jersey, and when ye are bolloxed, stick up your hand and we'll take you off. Plenty of lads on the sideline to do a job for ya ...'

*

Here's a story my auld fella told me about the legendary Matt Connor of Offaly and how Matt trained outside Eugene McGee's well-run Offaly camp. It tells you all you need to know about how much the lifestyle of inter-county stars has changed in recent times.

During the early 1980s my father was living in Dublin, in Ferguson Road, Drumcondra, sharing a house with Matt. During this time the faithful supporters were living their glory days, and a lot of it was due to the raw talent of 'the Thresher' (as Matt was known) between the white lines.

Dad would be sitting on the couch having a cup of scald after work, and Matt would come down the stairs wearing an old pair of runners, an O'Neill's in his hand. 'Joe,' he'd say, 'I'm running down to Na Fianna's pitch in Mobhi Road to do a few laps and have a kick-around. Any chance you'd follow me down in a half-hour, so I can take a few shots on ya?'

'No bother, Thresher. I'll be down soon.'

So off Matt would go, running along the road, soloing with his left, then his right, all the while jinxing between the telegraph poles along the footpath! Dad never played football at the top level, so he was amazed to see what Matt could do with a ball in hand: the man was a pure genius.

Dad often described to me how Matt would place the ball on the edge of either sideline, about sixty yards out. He'd shout at my auld lad, who'd be gathering the balls for Matt behind the goals.

'Right, Big Joe, left or right peg? Inside or outside of the foot?'

'Ah, Jaysus, whichever, Matt. Just hurry up ta fuck. I'm feckin' freezin' here!'

'Right, so,' says Matt, and he'd swing the ball straight over the black spot with a flick of his left peg!

One particular day Matt asked my dad to stand in the middle of the goalposts and not to move left or right. 'Stand dead still, Joe.'

While Matt was placing the ball on the penalty spot, and peeking at Dad with deadly concentration, my auld lad was getting very paranoid and felt a bit

If you kick that anywhere near my bollox I'll give you a kick in the arse!

THE STORY OF THE LEGENDARY
MATT CONNOR

intimidated. 'Matt, I'm warning you: if you kick the ball at my bollox, or anywhere near them, I'll give you a kick in the arse!'

'Ha, I won't, Horse, don't worry. Now don't move.' Matt walked back about three steps, took one last look at his target and *bang*!

The ball, according to my auld lad, came at him with a spin and a bend, crashing through a hole in the net no bigger than a dinner plate right behind him.

'Connor, ya auld snake, ya! Were you trying to fuckin' hit me or what!'

'No, I had planned to put it between your legs, all right, but when I noticed the hole in the net behind ya I thought that would be a better target.'

My auld man didn't realise at the time that he was kicking around with one of the greatest players ever to have graced Croke Park. Dad just thought of him as a friend who was 'a bit of craic and handy at the auld football'.

After the kick-abouts they'd call in to the Cat and Cage on the way home for a few pints of black. The die-hard GAA auld lads at the bar would often ask Matt plenty of questions. 'Will Offaly stop Kerry this year, Matt?'

'They will, Tommy, if they supply me with enough ball.' All the type of banter that goes on in all pubs around the country.

Back then, there was no such thing for players as Pilates classes, Bikram yoga, top-class diets or any of that craic: it was just training with your county two nights during the week, playing a game at the weekend and making a holy show of your friend down on the local GAA pitch on the off days.

It's such a pity that this naturally gifted footballer met with a bad car accident that ended his football career at twenty-four years of age. God knows what he would have gone on to achieve in the game. Well, my auld lad, for one, was delighted to have had the chance to run after many a ball that Matt curled over the black spot below in Na Fianna's GAA pitch in Mobhi Road.

*

Some chance you'd see Conor McManus or Diarmuid Connolly soloing a ball down the road these days. The difference in commitment among inter-county players nowadays is clear from this modern schedule.

Monday. Recovery session. Swimming, yoga, ice baths—followed by the best food known to man.

Tuesday. Field session. Timed sprints, with exact recovery, designed to suit match scenario, followed by the backs and forwards breaking into separate groups to practise specific plays. Session finished off with fifteen minutes on kick-out strategy: '$x + yz$, divided by the square root of M = retain our own kick-outs and puck-outs.'

Wednesday. Gym session. Specific programme for each individual player, some gaining muscle, others shredding for speed. Each drill will concentrate on specific muscles in the body.

Thursday. Field session. Working on various plays for the weekend's game—sweepers, maulers, runners, ball-carriers, retaining the ball, moving at pace, off the shoulder, retreating back in numbers ... Followed by the best food known to man!

Friday. Weight-training. Afterwards, massages and swimming.

Saturday. Light kick-around and some intense stretching, conducted by a highly qualified strength-and-conditioning coach.

Sunday. Match day. Throw-in is at 3 p.m. Meet at 10:30 a.m. for breakfast, followed by intense meetings. Get a top-of-the-range bus to the ground, with lunch ready on arrival. Another tactical chat. Start to get ready an hour before the match. Get well fed after the match, then home for a protein shake and some foam-rolling.

That's the proof, right there, that the GAA player nowadays is as much a professional as anyone playing rugby or soccer at the highest level. Well, bar the monster bank balance, that is!

April

April is a big month on the club scene, with most counties playing their first round of championship. Whatever it is about the first round, the buzz in every club is savage. The slogging is done, the friendlies and league matches have been played, the evenings are getting brighter and the pitch is getting a bit harder.

Everyone is gearing towards the big game. I can guarantee you that there won't be too many players missing from training the week of champo. You'll be sure to have the few heads pop out from the woodwork—lads you haven't seen since mid-February. They try to tiptoe into the dressing-room in the week of championships, head down, and go on out to the pitch unnoticed—no chance in a dressing-room full of lads in slagging form before the weekend's big match.

'Ha! Good man, Seánie. Nice to see ya, the week that's in it. Did ya forget we also train in late February and March?'

'Ah, no, I've been flat-out working the past couple of weeks—haven't had a chance to get down.'

'Would you stop! Working, me bollox. You just glued yourself to the Champions League mid-week and couldn't be arsed coming training. I know what you're like!'

This fella will expect game-time on Sunday but will be left on the bench. He'll be so pissed off that he won't even shower after the game. He'll curse and blind the manager and selectors.

'Them boys haven't a fuckin' clue how to pick a team. Whatever about not starting me because I've missed a few weeks' training, but to bring Snickers on ahead of me is an absolute joke. He's completely useless!'

He'll be blind to the fact that he hasn't put in the effort over the previous few weeks, as everyone else has. You'd think he'd knuckle down and come to training in the coming weeks, to try and get back into the starting fifteen, but these lads are the complete opposite: he won't be seen again at training until it's a lovely sunny evening, in mid-June or July, and he fancies a run-around!

*

The 'county men' will be back in town the week of the first round of club champ, sporting their flashy new county gear. The younger members of the panel tend to get a bit shy when the county men are about, but the older lads, who've been playing with them since they were nippers, don't show all that much respect—especially the thick fella who is 'club before county' to the core.

'Well, men, I was at that league game last week. What kind of a team had ye out? Brutal! It's worse you're getting: you're better off back training with us full time—only wasting your time, in with that county set-up!'

This fella will let on he's just having a sneer, but a good part of him would be deadly serious, partly because he was never good enough to play county himself, so he likes being ratty to the county players.

*

One important thing you'll notice in every dressing-room the week of champ is the new haircuts. It's a tradition now, at this stage.

The 'champo haircut': boyos wanting to look as slick as possible for the big day. Your standard country-wide champo haircut is

- nice and tight around the back and sides;
- blended in perfectly;
- given a stylish curvy fringe;
- gelled nicely before you leave the house for the big game.

Look good, feel good, play good!

THE GUY WITH THE
CHAMPO HAIRCUT

This is most often sported by the younger brigade of the team, with their motto 'Look good, feel good, play good!'

*

What's great about the first round of champ is that even the teams who have *zero* chance of winning a county championship, come October, are hyped to the nines for the first round. Most club teams train on Tuesdays and Thursdays, but before the first round of champ on the Sunday there will be a kick-about. The team is named on the Friday or Saturday.

'Right, boys, nobody has worked as hard as you have since January. Now go out there and prove it tomorrow.'

*

Players will debate over what boots to wear. 'Mouldies or studs, lads?' The raw full-back would usually have one pair of boots with the two-inch studs screwed into them! Up the other end of the field, the stylish free-taker could have up to three pairs in his bag on any given day.

When you go back over the past fifty years of the GAA, probably the most common boot you'll see is the Puma King—the old reliable wheels. Rumour has it there's a hurler from Co. Wicklow who got eight seasons out of the one pair—as solid a boot as you'll come across. Nowadays you have top-of-the-range boots, at €200 plus, that wouldn't last a kick-around on a wet evening in January.

The club groundsman

Clubs generally host championship matches themselves. Two teams either side of the county come to the club to play out their champo match. Clubs take a lot of pride in receiving teams and want to make sure that their pitch and grounds are in pristine condition.

This is where the infamous club groundsman is in full swing. Every club has this man—a thick man, to say the least. He treats the pitch like a family member. It takes a very brave bunch of young lads to be caught playing 'heads and volleys' in the goalmouth at any time of the year, but when the club is hosting a big championship match that weekend he's a different animal.

Your typical groundsman has the following features. As well as having the dirtiest pair of oil-rigged hands you're ever likely to come across—long, pointy fingernails; the lot!—he'll have on

- 🏐 a pair of ragged auld trousers;

- 🏐 an old shirt he once wore to a family wedding;

- 🏐 a very old pair of golf shoes, with the spikes taken off;

- 🏐 a twenty-year-old peaked cap with a very worn-looking *Lanzarote* printed on it—the same hat he bargained with a 'lucky, lucky' fella for on the beaches of Spain fifteen years earlier.

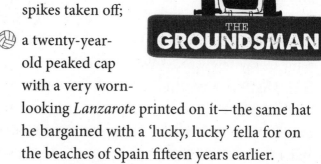

THE **GROUNDSMAN**

A very solid clubman—but he's one man you don't want to see angry.

The speech you have to listen to after a championship defeat

Preparing for the first round of championship is always great. You never prepare to be beat, of course: all the talk at training in the lead-up is how you're going to win the game. Obviously, everyone can't win the first round, and we've all been in a dressing-room after a loss. It's not a nice place to be: heads down, no talking, lads traipsing in and out of the shower—zero craic in the air. Everyone just wants to get the hell out of there and home to the house or the pub to hide. The last thing you want to hear is the opposing team's manager coming in to tell you how good a battle it was, how tough the game was—blah, blah, blah.

He'll make a little knock on the door and come in, taking off his hat, or something stupid like that. 'Sorry, men,' he'll say. 'I know you all must be devastated. Trust me: we know how it feels. I just want to say few words. You're a fantastic bunch of lads. That was a very tough match out there—could have went either way. We just got a couple of lucky breaks, I suppose. You're a real credit to your club, and I have no doubt you'll bounce back from this and be there or thereabouts next day out. Good luck, and all the best.'

They do mean well, I suppose, but everyone in the dressing-room is just sitting there thinking, Please, just shut up ta fuck and get out. It's a lot like the three cheers for the losing team after a final. The captain of the winning team will announce, 'And, last but not least, three cheers for ...' Now, that is torture, having to stand there and listen to that after losing a final—a match you put everything into before the game. I would say that nobody would care or object if they scrapped that tradition. It only annoys the life out of the losing team, and the winning captain doing it always feels like an eejit!

*

The inter-county league finals will be run off in April. They will be taken seriously, with championship only around the corner. Most teams will be showing their full deck of cards at this stage of the league: the team that starts the league decider won't be a million miles off the one that will feature in the first round of the provincial championships, so the league finals will be helter-skelter championship pace!

May

Inter-county friendlies

A lot of inter-county friendlies take place in May. Many clubs have official opening matches, with two nearby counties taking each other on. These are generally decent matches, as no great pressure is on either team, which means they tend to 'go at it'.

It's the same with clubs: each county would be looking further afield in order to test themselves against other club teams in various counties. These friendlies can often be great, high-scoring matches; they can also be great for the odd scuffle or two, because the referees can be a little bit more lenient with the whistle and the cards. Counties can try to lay down a marker in case they run into each other in Croke Park later on that summer.

*

I remember a so-called friendly I played in with my own club. It makes for a good story, with a few familiar GAA names involved.

There's this tournament that my club, Donaghmore-Ashbourne, play in every summer. It's hosted by the Garristown GAA club in Co. Dublin. Two clubs from Co. Meath and two from Co. Dublin play each other for a place in the final. Tournament games tend to be a bit more easy-going than, say, league or championship matches. In other words, you can get away with the odd late tackle or frontal shoulder. It's a great game to play in, because the ref is always local, very laid back and, let's just say, not too fond of blowing the whistle or taking out his notebook.

Well, one year we met Ballymun Kickhams in the final. They are, as you probably know, a very formidable outfit, and they're a bunch of lads I'd have plenty of respect for. We had two serious battles with them that year, eventually losing to them by a point in a replay. But it was the drawn game that left its mark!

We both fielded as strong an outfit as possible, in both games, because we had the quarter-finals of our county championships coming up. Both managers wanted to use this as an opportunity to have a serious test, in preparation. As the old saying goes, 'A good competitive game beats five training sessions,' and, by Jaysus, was this 'friendly' competitive!

About ten minutes into the drawn game their midfielder Barry McCarthy—brother of James, the Dublin all-Ireland winner—was throwing his weight around. I suddenly heard my manager, Andy McEntee (the present Meath senior football manager, and a top man), roar from the sideline, 'Roryyyy! *Roryyy!* Number eight! Number eight!' He gave me a very stern look, as much as to say, It's a tournament game; he's bullying a few of your team-mates. Sort that out whatever way necessary!

I gave him the salute, just like a solider would give his lieutenant when he orders him into battle! The next ball I gathered off our corner-back, I see Barry, a top bloke, coming towards me. I stuck up the elbow, as you do, and caught him straight in the snot machine.

Suddenly all hell broke loose. While myself and Barry were exchanging fists, wasn't half the sideline en route to the royal rumble. My auld lad was attempting to jump the fence, and a well-known local dog was barking at the banter he was witnessing.

One of our supporters, a clubman to the core, ran from his car, which was parked the far end of the field. But by the time he got to the row it was broken up. Even if it hadn't been, he was that out of breath from galloping up the sideline that he wouldn't have been much use to us!

The bould Philly McMahon of Ballymun Kickhams made his way up from corner-back and managed to get a couple of lads into a knot, with his martial-arts skills. In fairness to him, he was one of the few lads who tried to split it up, thanks be ta Jaysus: nobody would fancy a slap off the roaming Dublin corner-back.

Then there was the Ballymun water boy who ran in and 'introduced' his half-full bottles to a few of our lads, from whatever angle he found possible.

The Dublin legend Barney Rock was also along the sideline, because his son Dean was playing for the 'Mun. Barney would be far too cute and experienced to get involved in that auld nonsense, so he sat back and enjoyed the bit of scalping that was going on.

After about thirty seconds of hell-for-leather fighting, it settled down, and both myself and Barry were called over by the ref, who had just witnessed the best bit of entertainment he'd seen since *Rumble in the Bronx*. Myself and Barry were standing there absolutely shattered tired and panting away. 'He was acting da bollox first, ref,' says me, trying to prove my case.

The ref was half trying not to laugh as he took out the notebook. 'Right, lads,' he says, 'I have no choice but to send the pair of ye off, or I'll be shot. But I know ye both have championship matches coming up, so I'll leave this incident out of the match report.'

'Ah, fair play to ya, ref,' says the pair of us as we shook hands. We nodded at each other and made our way to the sideline to cheer our teams on for the rest of the game.

*

I do believe that most GAA followers love a good row at a game. It gets the adrenaline going in all the supporters. I was only a gossoon when Meath and Mayo went hammer and tongs in the 1996 all-Ireland final, and it was very enjoyable to watch—even if it wasn't the greatest message for them to be getting across. There's just something about a good row on a field. As long as nobody gets seriously injured, a good row every now and again is no harm.

Keeping hydrated

You're nearly always guaranteed a few very warm days in May, and this prompts managers to break out the rant about keeping hydrated. You're told from the age of thirteen that the body needs enough water, especially when the weather is warm. But managers always have to stress this at training. The standard speech goes something like this:

> 'Right, lads, the forecast is for very humid, warm weather in the next few days, so I want you drinking at least three litres of water a day. If ye

can at all, avoid the sun too: don't be out lying round getting the body burnt off yourselves. Your piss should be as clear as crystal, do youse hear me? Water, water, water! Keep sipping all day.'

Some chance of the farmers staying out of the sun when there's footing to be done on the bog. You can see the farmers a mile away coming down to club training—head, neck and arms red raw, with the rest of the body a milk bottle.

The townies v. the country players

In the GAA world there's a huge divide between the townies and the country men. Now, I'm not talking about Dubs versus culchies. In every county there are the one or two townie teams that everyone wants to beat. They're generally full of talent, but they can't click—too many egos—and a lot of the time they'll have a good scatter of lads on the county panel.

Here's exactly what you'll find in every townie team:

- They will do plenty of shouting and roaring on the field during a match.

- They will be full of egos.

- They will have the best of gear.

- The will have fancy haircuts.
- They do not like when you get 'stuck in' to them.

The hardy country boyos are a different breed altogether. Generally, their club will be from an area where everyone knows everyone. These are traits you'll find in every country team:

- They won't be the most talented group.
- They will be a very hard team to beat.
- They will be *raw*.
- There will be plenty of lads on the team who would have done a twelve-hour shift on the farm before the game.
- They might have the bare fifteen, but it's fifteen lads who will give 110 per cent.

It's not just the players who are different. The manager of the townie team will give a speech like this:

'Right, men, we know what we're getting with these. Do not get involved: they're going to try and drag us down to their level. We don't want this game to be turned into a dogfight. Don't retaliate: that's what they want. Let the referee do his job. It's what he's there for. We will do the talking on the pitch, and on the scoreboard. Do I make myself clear?'

The townies will leave the dressing-room in an orderly fashion, focused on the job in hand.

In the opposite dressing-room you'll have a completely different approach to the game. The manager of the country team will give a speech like this:

'Right, lads, stand up there and link each other. We know what we're getting from these boys today. If we stand back and admire them they'll walk all over us; but we all know they're fucking soft. The first chance you get I want you to let your man know you're there. I don't care how you do it: just don't get caught by the ref. Once we get in their faces they won't want to know about it. You know and I know that they hate playing us. Well, let's make this a dogfight, because I can guarantee you they will blink first. Leave everything on the pitch, lads. We die for that badge on your jersey, and if a row breaks out, one in, we're all in. So get out there and get stuck in.'

The manager will finish his speech by hitting the door or the table in front of him a couple of boxes.

The country men will then take the hinges off the door as they run out onto the field, ready to do whatever they have to do to get the victory!

*

During these matches there's often plenty of argy-bargy on the sidelines between supporters—woeful shouting and roaring altogether. This is the kind of thing you'll have seen if you've ever been to one of these matches.

A hardy corner-back from the country team would sense that the townies are starting to get a bit of a run on them. They might have got three or four points in a row, so the corner-back knows he needs to 'stop their rhythm'. In his own thoughts that means, Right, I need to nail someone here.

Before long, a ball would be kicked into a townie corner-forward—a chap on the minor county team, and a real gem of a prospect. Just as he tries to gain possession, the corner-back, a wearing-no-gloves-on-a-wet-day type of a fella, will come in from behind and hit him a 'clip on the ear'. The ref's whistle will sound.

'Ah, come on, ref. I was going for the ball. It was there to be won ...'

Handbags will break out. Without doubt, the country men will be in there throwing shoulders. Then it spills onto the sideline ...

Country supporter: That's the boy, Micky— great hit. Come on, lads, get stuck in to the softies.

Townie supporter: Referee! Where's your red! Number 2, you're an absolute disgrace, ya dirty thug, ya!

Country supporter: Who are you calling a thug! That was a fair hit.

Townie supporter: Fair hit, my arse—disgrace of a tackle.

Country supporter: Ah, sure youse are nothing but a bunch of windy townies.

Townie supporter: Good man. Have youse not to head off now and cut some turf?

The corner-back will get a yellow card, but it will be a yellow 'well worth getting', because it will put the fear into the townies.

No matter how many points ahead the townies are, the speech at half time will be:

'Okay, men, we're well ahead here, but you know these lads won't go away: they're only interested in fighting, so let the ref do his job, and keep the mouth shut.'

The country speech at half time will be another long rant.

'Right, lads, they got a run on us early on, but we aren't dead and buried yet. No matter what happens out here we never give up. Keep in their faces, lads. As ye know, these bunch are well capable of bottling it here: if we get a sniff of a chance, go for it. Leave everything on the field.'

Once the townie slickers start to pull away in the game, that's when the yellow cards come hot and heavy. The country lad's attitude is 'They might hammer us, but I'll nail one or two of them,' and the game becomes a mess. It's always the way once a townie team get a run on the country rivals. If the shoe was on the other foot, and there was only a point or two in it with a few minutes to go, you can bet your bottom dollar the country men would get over the line by a point or two.

Even after games there's a difference in how the townies and country lads go about their business. The country lads will head off together to their local pub to have a few pints and chat about the game. The townies might have one or two together, but other groups of friends will come calling, and they'll scatter off one by one. There's just a stronger bond between country teams and clubs than at clubs in big towns. That has been the way for years, and long will it continue.

June

Off to the States

You'd think that June, at the middle of the Irish summer, would be the best time to play most matches, but in fact it's one of the quietest months on the club scene. Every fixture throughout the country is held up because of 'the county'.

This is the most frustrating part of being a club player. Fixtures are heaped on you once the county team is knocked out of the all-Ireland race, but during probably the best month for weather in Ireland you have fuck-all matches to play. Lads get a pain in their hole hanging around for the summer, playing Mickey Mouse fixtures and training for nothing serious in the near future.

Just this year (2017) the Club Players' Association was formed to try and tackle this issue of 'fixing the fixtures' for the club player. I hope it takes off, as it's badly needed to keep the club game flowing. What happens in the summers nowadays is that many of the young bucks—mainly university students who don't fancy hanging around their towns and villages for the summer, waiting on potential fixtures—decide to hit the United States for the summer on a J-1 visa.

'I plan on going to New York, Boston or San Francisco for the summer.' This is not what your manager wants to hear after a training session in late May or early June.

They would already have asked the question at the pre-season meeting in January. 'Right, lads, I know a couple of you college folks might be interested in going to America on the J-1 this summer, so if anyone here is thinking of heading away, come to me after the meeting for a chat.'

Now, do you think there would be a queue of people lined up to tell the manager their plans? No chance! Very few managers are going to be encouraging you to go—I'll tell you that for nothing.

It's highly unlikely that such a conversation would go anything like this:

Player: Good man, John. I'm going to head over to Boston for the summer—great opportunity to see the States.

Manager: That's no bother, Seánie. I think you're dead right. Sure who cares about the club's chances of winning the championship: we're only in this for the bit of craic and to keep fit. You head off there and be sure to ask the rest of the lads: one or two might be interested as well. You'll have a right bit of craic over there.

Player: That's sound of ya, John. Will do.

If only it were that easy. But 99 per cent of players won't breathe a word of their plans to the manager in January, because you'll already be putting yourself on the back foot with the manager: you'll be giving him an easy excuse not to start you in the first few games.

'To be out straight with ya, Tommy,' he'd say, 'I won't be starting you, because it's not fair on the other lads, who'll be here all summer. If I start you I'll have to change the team, either way, when you're gone.' This is a good bullshit excuse for a manager to use if they're just pissed off that you're 'letting down the parish' by heading stateside and they want to punish you in any way they can. So they'll just drop you from the get-go.

Let's be honest: if you had a chance to spend a couple of months living it up in New York, Boston, San Francisco or Chicago, would you turn it down? Bollox would ya! While you debate with yourself the pros and cons, I'll list them here for you.

Pros

- Simply having the craic in America for two months.

- Your flights, accommodation and job are sorted for you.

- It's 30 degrees every day.

- You will meet so many new friends.

- You will 99 per cent likely pull an American on your travels, as it's a fact that they love the auld Irish accent.

- You get a chance to play football with lads from all over Ireland.

- You go on the beer after every match.

- Barbecues are arranged most evenings.

Cons

🏐 You will more than likely miss maybe *one* championship match.

🏐 You will miss Mammy's cooking and her washing your clothes.

THE END.

Seriously, is it much of a decision to make? The only people within the club who hold it against you are the thick, old-school auld lads—who no doubt would be gonzo for it if they were fifty years younger! Oh, and the older, wiser heads on the team—the men who are settled and probably have a nipper, or one on the way. They'll also try make you feel bad, but they're just sick that they aren't in your shoes.

When you do build up the courage to break the news to your bainisteoir after training on the Thursday night, the conversation will actually go like this:

Player: John, can I chat to you for a minute?

Manager: Ah, good man, Decy. No bother. What can I do for you? Jesus, you're flying at the minute. Fair play to you! [This is not at all what you want to hear from him, right before you break his heart!]

Player: Listen, John, I'm heading off to Boston for the summer. I'm after getting looked after, big time. It's something I really want to do.

Manager: You're going fucking *where*! [His humour changes in a heartbeat, as he stares into your eyes.]

Player: I'm going with a couple of lads from college to play football with Monaghan.

Manager: Ya are in your bollox. We have important league games coming up, and we need you. So go on away with that nonsense.

Player: Honestly, it's booked. I'm heading Saturday morning. I'll be back for championship.

Manager: Saturday morning, and you tell me now, two days before you head off. That's some respect to show me and your team-mates. You can go, but you won't be playing for this team again as long as I'm in charge.

It's 100 per cent certain that Decy will be full-forward and scorer-in-chief come the quarter-final of the championship, and he'll be one good performance away from anyone remembering, or even caring, that he went to the States on a J-1 for the summer. *Fact.*

July

The month of July in the GAA is all go on the county front: you have the provincial finals throughout the country and a few very juicy qualifier matches. I think it's fair to say that the provincial championship structure has run its race: it's an old but, for a long time, very successful format in the GAA.

Back in the 90s, and in previous years, it was a knockout series that did create a great buzz: you lose your first game and you're gone—no ifs or buts. So each game had a lot riding on it, and you were under massive pressure. The whole six months of hard work was down the swanny if you were beaten. They were unbelievably exciting games for the supporters to go to and enjoy.

In 2001 the big guns brought in the back-door system to give teams a second bite at the cherry, and it has to be said that it has been a great success. Some teams (Tyrone, Kerry, Kilkenny) have benefited greatly from the back door and have used it to go on and lift the Sam Maguire Cup and the Liam MacCarthy Cup.

It can create a great buzz in counties if your team goes on a run: it means games week after week throughout the country during the summer, and fans get the chance to explore different parts of the country and to have a few large bottles and sing songs in the beer gardens wherever they go—great auld craic.

Wouldn't it be great to see the provincial system given the heave-ho and to have a format similar to the Champions League in soccer? Take the National Leagues, for instance: each and every weekend you have the same calibre of teams facing off, and you're always guaranteed a couple of cracking matches. Apart from one or two good games during the summer, the best matches are played during the league. So why not mix everything up and have games like this each weekend? It would be great to see the GAA move in that direction in the coming years.

The trip up to Croke Park for the day

When your county is playing above in Croke Park on a big championship Sunday, it can be a great day out.

It's the morning of the 'big game' in Croke Park, and in counties Donegal, Kerry, Galway, Limerick, Derry and Tipperary the die-hards awake from their leabas. The full fry is a guarantee, with a solid three cups of tae. The papers are read, and the chit-chat about the game begins.

'Jesus, we'd better push up on Cluxton's kick-outs and really take it to the Dubs.'

Off you head to Mass for a quick prayer, and then all roads lead to Croker. The drive up to the Big Smoke is always very exciting.

'I wonder will they go with the team he named ...'

'Ah, sure he can't. We'll be ate in the full-back line if he does.'

'Joe Canning is key. If he shows up we'll surely win.'

You might stop for a toilet break on the way down, and there'd be the buzz among your own supporters as you're drying your hands.

'Well, Mick, will we win, ya think?'

'It'll be tough. Them boys are a solid auld outfit. Sure we'll give it a lash.'

When you get near Croker you can nearly smell the excitement in the air. It's unreal—colours everywhere. You spend twenty minutes looking for a parking spot. Once you find one, it's time to open up the boot and tear into a few ham sambos and a flask of beautiful tea. 'Jaysus, lads, that's a mighty day for a match—powerful!' But when it's time to top up your 'pay and display' you're not too happy. 'Isn't that some fucking joke, lads, €3.50 per hour, and I'll be here half the day with the double-header on—dirty hoors.'

As you head down Whitworth Road, the noise of Croker is getting louder. 'Get your hats, scarfs and headbands—three for a fiiiverrr,' roar the locals at their stands, trying to flog a bit of colour to the travelling countryfolk.

You go in through the turnstiles of Croker, pick up a programme, walk up the steps and get that buzz when you see the pitch: the shiver runs down your spine, and you're wishing you could be out there.

After you sit down and flick through the programme, you keep an eye on both teams in the warm-up, to see if you can pick up on anything strange: a late inclusion to either team, or an unusual warm-up routine. You roar like fuck when the players walk past you during the parade, all thirty players pumped up, with their chests out, and hopping off the ground. Then it's time for the national anthem: up you stand, hands behind the back, and you belt out 'Amhrán na bhFiann' word for word, proud as punch.

The ball is thrown in, and we're off. If you're playing the Dubs, each score you get you'll turn and shake your fist at Hill 16. 'Now that'll shut yiz up, yiz bolloxes!'

Your heart is close to exploding for seventy-plus minutes: the ups and downs of every minute, the 'will we, won't we'. At the final whistle, if your team is on the right side of the scoreboard it's mayhem; if not, it's depression.

After the game, if you're staying up in the Big Smoke for the night, you'll head off for a skip of pints and a dissection of the game, play for play.

Or else it's back to the car, hoping not to find it clamped! The motor will be full of chat if you win, or extremely silent and pissed off if you lose. But, either way, you can't beat a summer's day out in Páirc an Chrócaigh.

Planning holidays

The club scene in July is fairly quiet. You'd think it would be a great time for heading off on holidays, but it isn't easy trying to pencil in a week for a holiday when you're a GAA head. The poor club player is hanging around all summer waiting on the county team to see how far they get: once they're out of the all-Ireland race the club championship will be landed on you the very next weekend.

As well as making it impossible to plan holidays, this can also be tough going when you're in a relationship. Your partner is hounding you at the beginning of the year to name a date when you can go away for a bit of sun together. This is when the shit hits the fan and things gets tricky: you can't actually give an exact time, because of the way the club players are shafted with structures. The conversation in every such household early January is as follows.

Sarah: Mark, I'm looking at Tenerife here for the first week in February. There won't be any matches on, will there?

Mark: Eh, I'd say we'll have the first round of the league then—don't want to miss that and lose my jersey.

Sarah: Okay, what about the second week of April? There's a good deal here for Lanzarote.

Mark: Can't. It's the first round of championship.

Sarah: My God, you're a pest. What about the first week of August? It's more expensive, but—

Mark: Can't, because I doubt the county team will get too far this year, so there will defo be championship around then.

Sarah: Mother of God. Well, then I have a place here for a week in October—not ideal, but the weather should be okay.

Mark: Nope. If we reach the county final it will be around then.

Sarah: Mark, I'm with you the past ten years and you have never *been* in a county final!

Mark: I know, but this could be our year. What about December?

Sarah: December, December ... Mark, are you having a laugh? The sooner you give up that football the better. We never get to go anywhere.

*

No doubt about it, that's the conversation in so many houses around the country every year. There's no good time to go away for a bit of sun and a few cocktails, as the season for the club player is all over the shop. The sooner it changes, the better.

August

August is when the real stuff starts to happen on the county front. It's the famous August bank holiday bonanza in Croker. Some would say it's the real start of the football championship, because everything up to then has been landslide victories and plenty of piss-poor matches.

On the hurling front we have both all-Ireland semi-finals. And in camogie and women's football it's 'squeaky-bum time' for the big hitters.

You're always guaranteed one, if not two, top-class matches at the August bank holiday weekend, as the big guns collide. It's the first time all year that you have the potential for a full, rip-roaring Croke Park. It's nearly always a good weekend for weather, so a lot of supporters around the country flock to the Big Smoke.

The culchie's guide to Dublin on match day

There's a fear of the Big Smoke whenever the 'countryfolk' come to play Dublin during the summer in the championship action in Croke Park. Below is a guideline that most households more than fifty

THE CULCHIE'S GUIDE TO
DUBLIN ON MATCH DAY

miles outside Dublin hand out at the kitchen table while having breakfast on the day of the 'big game above in Dublin'. This is to make sure that everyone is clear on what to do and what not to do.

- Be very wary of the price of drink: you could pay up to €7 for a single pint. Naggins and flagons advised.

- Do not, and I repeat, *do not* make eye contact with anyone in a Dublin jersey, especially groups of lads 'drinking cans'.

- No matter how friendly anyone may seem, everyone is out to do you in Dublin. They see us as easy targets, so heads down.

◉ If you're driving make sure you park in a 'professional' car park. It might be €20 an hour, but it's not worth the risk to leave your car at the mercy of a man from Dublin. Nine times out of ten you will return from Croke Park to find your car on blocks, with your four wheels gone, and that's at best. If you're a bit of a rebel and want to take a risk parking in the street, be sure to give a few bob to any young lads who offer to mind the car for you. Otherwise you will find that your wing mirror has magically disappeared when you return to the car.

◉ Always bring a packed lunch: don't leave the house without at least two sliced pans full of ham and cheese, one flask of tea and six bottles of Lucozade. You will be charged a small fortune for a burger or a sandwich above in Dublin.

◉ If you are 'on the piss' for the day, make sure to be in the queue for Copper Face Jacks no later than 10 p.m. in order to avoid being refused. If you get refused it will ruin your whole night, as the main reason for hanging around Dublin after games is to hear the Saw Doctors in Copper's at 3 a.m.

🏐 All under-12s must hold Mammy's hand at all times—no exceptions. That is unless you need a piss: in that case Mammy will wait for you outside the toilets.

🏐 No matter how hot a day it is, and how good the forecast was, always bring a jacket with you, as you wouldn't know what kind of weather it is up in Dublin. You can always tie your jacket round your waist.

🏐 If you're over the age of sixty-five, make sure to pack your radio for listening to the game on RTÉ while watching it, as you will be charged up to five times the standard price for a radio in or around Croke Park.

*

On the club scene, reaching the month of August means that it's getting to the business end in most counties—apart from the likes of Dublin and Kilkenny, whose club teams are shafted by having to wait on the county team to finish up the season, which is always close to September! So you have the club players from the stronger counties playing the most important games of their season in the muck and the shite. Makes sense ... I don't think so!

In August you have the J-1 heads crawling back into club training with their tails between their legs, after a couple of months drinking, working, more drinking, acting the maggot and playing the odd bit of GAA here and there! They arrive back with tanned legs, the sleeveless jerseys and the free socks and togs on them.

Sneery selector: Good man, Tom. Ya made your way back to us in one piece, I see. Ya must have spent a fortune on the fake tan before ya left—big brown head on ya!

Tom: Ha, would ya stop! Sure it was 28 degrees every day over there—was sweating me bollox off on the sites.

Sneery selector: Yeah, I'd say you were, all right—more like breastfeeding the shovel, talking through your arse all day!

Tom: Ah, well, sure I was paid well to breastfeed a shovel, so!

Generally, the manager would give these travelling buckos the cold shoulder for a week or two, but once the big game comes along, the peace will be made. The auld men who were slagging the player for leaving the club for a bit of banter stateside will be the same fellas licking his arse and sending a pint of porter in his direction after he plays a blinder, guiding the club through to the quarter-final of the club championship.

'Fair play to ya, Tom boy, you were outstanding today. You were badly missed when you were on your travels. Great to have ya back in the club colours ...'

Dressing-rooms now v. thirty years ago

I've often thought to myself how much the game has come on since, say, the 1980s, and there's no better way to sum up the difference than to look at the culture change inside the dressing-room.

BACK IN 1985
IN THE DRESSING ROOM

Back in 1985 you'd walk into club training and find

- lads turning up to training in a pair of dirty working jeans, a horrible rolled-up shirt and a pair of dodgy black boots;

- at least five players using a shopping bag as their gear bag;

- one lad getting the last few drags from a cigarette before heading out to train;

- every man wearing odd football socks;

- one pair of boots per man, per year and probably per career;

- a first-aid box consisting of a used bandage and a bottle of water;

- one fella walking around looking for his Mikasa gloves;

- no grips on anyone's hurl, and not a helmet to be seen.

'Raw' would be the only way to describe the characters in a dressing-room back then.

You walk into any club dressing-room now and it's like a different world. You're guaranteed to see

- lads arriving in skinny tracksuit bottoms, shiny runners and various styles of haircut;

- foam rollers scattered all over the floor;

- heaps and heaps of white wrist-tape;

- each player having two pairs of boots;

- each player having their initials on their training top;

- proper gear bags;

- three hurls with fancy grips on them;

IN THE DRESSING-ROOM
TODAY

- players rubbing Deep Heat on very minor injuries.

I tell ya, it's some difference, so it is. Not too many lads nowadays would have lasted in a dressing-room back in the 80s: the prima donnas were few and far between back then.

September

This is the month every inter-county player wants to be playing in—the month of the world-famous all-Ireland final, the day every young Irish person wants to be a part of, even if very few get to live the dream. Living it as a player must be unreal, but it isn't too bad living it as a supporter of your county. My Jaysus, what a day—and night—the all-Ireland final is ...

This is a typical final-day routine:

08:30. Up and out of bed—a slight headache from the few pints the night before, but the buzz of the day ahead will clear any hangover.

09:00. The biggest fry known to man.

10:00. Down to Mass for a prayer. 'Please let this be our day. Please, God, let this be our day.' To be said a hundred times throughout the service.

10:30. Half the parish discuss the match outside the church. ''Twill be tough, but if we take our scores I think we will win ...'

11:00. The final few prayers are said silently before you leave the house.

11:30. You're on the road and in as good a form as you can imagine. If your body was capable of doing backflips you'd be doing hundreds of them with the excitement.

13:00. You arrive in Dublin. The buzz, the colour and the excitement are in overdrive.

13:30. A couple of pre-match pints to settle the nerves and to enjoy the craic with your own and the opposition supporters. ''Tis our day, boy, 'tis our day.

I'm telling ya, now, 'tis our day—we're flying,' as you slap a random fellow-county man on the back as you leave the toilets.

14:30. You head into Croker to get some of the minor game.

15:15. The teams come running out from underneath the Hogan Stand to a deafening sound. You're roaring, shouting and waving your programme with sheer aggression and excitement. 'Hon, Mayo.' 'Up the Dubs.' 'Hon, Westmeath.' 'Up, Tipp.' 'C'mon, Tyrone.'

15:28. You sing every word of 'Amhrán na bhFiann' in your own way, with your hands behind your back and the chest out, at the top of your lungs—the way you think it sounds in your head. Completely wrong, more than likely.

15:30. The ball is in, and we're off. Like all GAA people, you turn into this crazy lunatic as the ball goes from end to end, yourself and the man beside you arguing over the referee's decisions.

'Ah, fuck's sake, ref. Blatant penalty.'

'Would you shut up! You haven't a clue.'

'I'll shut you up, very lively.'

'Go for it.'

But, like most solid GAA folk, this is as far as the row will go. You're both soon calmed down and getting stuck back in to the game.

16:05. The half-time whistle blows, and the crowd roars as the teams head back underneath the Hogan. You're bursting to go to the toilet, and it's a massive job. You dance around at the back of the queue, desperately needing to 'drain the spuds'. You eventually get into a wedged toilet, it's so packed. You squeeze in between two farmers and have the same conversation as the other 80,000 people in the stadium.

'Good game. Should be a great second half. All the best. Good luck.'

You get back to your seat, give the hands a quick rub of excitement and you're ready for the second half.

16:30. The teams are back out, and it's game on.

17:00. The last five minutes of an all-Ireland final can be a bundle of stress on the auld ticker. For many, this is everything: win and it's party time for the week; lose and it's post-mortems for the week.

17:07. The whistle sounds, and your county has done it. A wave of madness hits you. 'Yeooowww! Yeowww! we did it, ya fuckin' boy, ya'—as you hug an unknown fellow-county man in front of you. You leap around as your county's song is blared from the stadium speakers.

17:30. You shed a tear as your captain gives a rousing speech and lifts the Holy Grail.

18:00. From this time onwards the day starts to become a blur. You party the evening away in the pubs and bars of the capital, knowing that it's party time in your county for the week ahead.

*

On the Monday you head back for the homecoming, just about able to function. 'My God, lads, that was some session last night. It was bright when I left Copper's, dying.'

But you aren't missing the craic in your county town for love nor money, so it's home you go. The session and celebrating could go on for a week: that's why it's so special when your county does win the all-Ireland. The craic is hard to beat!

*

On the club scene in September, if your team is still involved, it's always good news. There's an old saying: 'If you have to switch the floodlights back on in the same calendar year, you know you're going well.' That's if you're *let* put the lights back on: most teams will have to spend a good part of the training session in poor light. As with most clubs, there will be arguments about putting on the lights too early.

'Tommy, Tommy, will ya go in there and switch on the lights?'

'Sure there's plenty of light left in the day,' says Tommy, the hungry bollox of a secretary, as if the money was coming out of his pocket. 'Would you not train a half hour early to save the lights coming on?' says Tommy.

The club is one game away from a county final, and here is the miserable hoor wanting to save few shillings!

*

At this time of year it's generally the semi-final stage in the club championship, so managers and players are starting to get excited about a potential county final. Every manager's speech in the week before the semi-final will be:

'Right, men, it's been a great year so far, but it won't be worth a shit unless we win on Sunday. We said at the start of the year that our goal was to make the county final, and we're one game away from that. Just one! So I want ya to eat, sleep and drink this panel for the next couple of weeks. No acting the bollox: we've too much to lose.'

There will always be a bite to training at this time of year, because few places will be up for grabs. A niggly row is no harm: a corner-back trying to break into the team will have no bother pulling the jersey off the talisman in a training game.

'Get your hands off me, Deano.'

'Ah, calm down, Seánie. What's wrong with ya? You'll be getting this treatment on Sunday.'

The truth of the matter is that managers love seeing a good row among the players at training. 'It's healthy,' as they say! If two lads have to be sent off in a training match in order to calm down, it means that the team are in a good place heading into the semi-final!

October

The month of October is all about the club action. By this stage the inter-county season is put to bed. On the club scene, if your club is still involved in the championship it generally means only one thing: *county final day*.

What a day for the parish! Once your club gets over the banana skin that is any semi-final and reaches the final, everywhere, from the smallest village to the biggest town, comes to a halt. It's time for the flags, the banners, the posters and the excitement. The build-up in any parish for a county final is always brilliant, from the buzz at training to the bit of new club gear you get the week of the game.

Generally, in the week of the county final you'll have a bit of a match on the Tuesday night, a lighter session involving tactics on the Thursday and a kick-around on the Saturday, before Sunday's showdown. The craic and excitement at training during this week is always through the roof. There won't be a single body late for training that week. In fact, you'll have most of the panel there a half hour before training, chatting and having the banter in the dressing-room.

You'll always get one chancer who hasn't been seen near training since the summer, but he's sure to land down with his gear bag the week of the final. He'll probably be a talented enough player, but he's never really arsed to go training, turning up only when it suits him. This fella doesn't want to miss the chance of a county medal, or the week on the beer that follows it. He'll sneak into the dressing-room on the Tuesday night, as unnoticed as he possibly can. But there's no chance a bunch of GAA lads will let him away with that.

'Would ya look at this cowboy! Good man, D'Arcy. Hardly back to training just for the bit of gear and to tog out Sunday, are ya?'

'Ah, no, I've been flat-out on the farm the past few months, so I haven't had a chance to train. I've been doing my own bit in the gym.'

'Would you ever fuck off with yourself!' says a lad in the far corner of the dressing-room, who's desperately holding on to the number 30 in the match-day programme—a useless hoor of a player, but he deserves a jersey on Sunday for all his time sitting on the bench and never missing a training session. 'If ya think you're taking my jersey on Sunday ya can go and ask my bollox,' he says as he brushes past him and out the door to the pitch.

*

Most nights during the year you can barely get lads to hang around after for the warm-down, but, bejaysus, the week of a county final there's no bother there. Not only will they warm down properly but they'll all fancy themselves as free-takers, as most of the team hang back to kick a few points or puck a few sliotars. Again the hungry auld secretary puts an end to that craic by switching off the floodlights.

'G'wan home ta Jaysus there, men. I want to lock this place up and go home and split a single Fig Roll with the missus over a shared teabag!'

*

The morning of the county final is some buzz. Nine-tenths of the players will have slept fuck-all the night before—tossing and turning in the bed, up and down the landing to the toilet about twenty times because of drinking a mental amount of water in order to be hydrated. When they're very close to nodding off they'll get a vision of themselves scoring the winning point, and the body will be full of adrenaline once again.

'Jesus Christ, God, just let me sleep. I want it to be morning.'

They'll get out of bed early. Even though the match isn't on till 3:30 that afternoon, they'll have the bag packed and checked a hundred times by 9 in the morning. In it they'll have two pairs of boots, cleaned for the first time; a brand-new pair of gloves, sponsored by the local plumber; new shorts and socks, still in the plastic; a fresh towel; and a lovely new raincoat.

All anyone on the panel wants to do is to get the ball thrown in, as the butterflies will be on a mad one in the tummy. You assemble at the club grounds, everyone edgy but excited—in fact, deep down they're shitting themselves—and it's off to the county grounds.

There will always be one lad who can't cope with the nerves: he's been up since 6 o'clock that morning, doing push-ups and punching a boxing bag. 'The first chance I get I'm going to take my man clean out of it with a shoulder.' He'll have been telling himself this all morning, and he'll be bouncing off lads on the team bus on the way to the match. There's a fair good chance this man will be either sent off or taken off at half time for being absolutely useless. Far, far too over-hyped!

Everyone gets togged out, and it's nearly time, so the manager gives the standard county final speech.

'This is it, men. Stand up and link each other. Today is our day. We've been training since last January for this moment. Remember all them dirty runs through the muck and the shite? That was all for today. Promise yourselves that you'll leave everything on the field. Die for that jersey on yer back ... '

Some lads will be nearly crying with the passion at this stage. Then he'll finish with 'Now get out there and win this championship!'

The whole dressing-room will let out a monster '*C'mon ta fuck, ladsss!*' as they burst out the door and onto the field.

The ups and downs of every county final will be played out. The final whistle is blown, you win and it's mayhem, which always consists of a huge pile-on in the middle of the field—players, management, the chairman, the water boys: the lot. The poor chap on the bottom of the pile will be flat out, pinching arses and legs to let people know he's seconds away from passing out.

If you lose the match, it's on the knees with devastation as you watch the other team jump with joy. All you want to do is crawl into a hole with a keg of porter.

Either way, both sets of players are going on the piss for a couple of days.

Celebrating a win

It really is some tradition the GAA has for celebrating county championship success. Every club that wins their respective championship goes full tilt on the celebrations. The standard few days after a memorable win will go as follows.

The Sunday after the match the whole parish will head back to the local village or town to welcome their heroes home. The team will be greeted with huge excitement. They'll more than likely be up on the back of a local man's lorry, parading down through the village, beeping, fog horns—the lot.

The clubhouse or local pub will be packed as the captain and his troops enter with the cup to a massive roar. 'Hon, ya fuckin' boy, ya! Yeoowww! Campeones, campeones, olé, olé, olé!'

The drink will continue long in to the early hours of Monday morning, each player getting slaps on the back from delighted and drunk supporters. The smoking area will be full of stories and chat about the final. 'You were unreal, Johnny.' 'No, you were unreal, Mackey.' 'No, you were unreal ...'

By 11 a.m. on Monday morning the lads, most often still in the club tracksuit, will make their way to the pub from house parties, from their own bed, and sometimes from someone else's bed, if they had a great match the day before! The form is unreal as the slap-up fry is put out in front of them.

One or two of the lads with the lesser amount of alcohol in the system will bring the cup round the local schools to inspire the next generation of parish legends.

The day is spent among the proper club folk and a few stragglers sculling pints while the game is shown on repeat all day. The craic is ninety. 'You didn't give him a sniff of the ball yesterday, Fozzy. If you don't get a call to the county panel now, after that performance, it'll prove that that bollox of a manager doesn't like this club.'

It's an old tradition that the losing team will join the winners for a few beers on the Monday night. I think this is brilliant, and it shows all that's great about the GAA—one big family—although tempers can spill over if the winning team has a sneery little bollox who likes waving the cup in the losing players' faces!

Unless you live a million miles away from Dublin, a bus will be called to bring your weary and drunken bodies up to the famous Copper Face Jacks to continue the banter.

The celebrations can often go on for the week, depending on how long your club has been starved of success and how seriously you plan on taking the provincial championship and the first step on the long road to Croke Park for St Patrick's Day!

When my own club won the Meath intermediate football championship in 2007 it was the first time we had won it in fifty-eight years. As you can imagine, there was great excitement. I was twenty, and I still remember clearly the celebrations that went on. I think I lived in my club tracksuit for the week, with sick on the T-shirt, not a care in the world. All the auld bucks of the club who longed for the day—they were throwing ya pints, and there were sing-songs, heart-to-hearts, trips to Copper's. I think anyone who has ever won a championship with their club will tell you that it's one of the best experiences of your life—memories that last for ever.

The Aussie Rules Series

THE
AUSSIE RULES SERIES

Also in the month of October you have the International Rules Series between Ireland and Australia. It began in 1984 and takes place every two years. This is a chance for the amateur sports-men of Gaelic football to pit themselves against the might of the professional Aussies.

The game is essentially Gaelic football, but you're allowed to rugby tackle your opponent when he has the ball. To say the Aussies were better at this is an understatement: Jaysus, they used to wrap ya up if ya were anyway near them, and welly ya to the floor.

Savages! There's been a fair few rows in the games: Peter Canavan of Tyrone and Graham Geraghty of Meath, to take two examples, have felt the full impact of the big Aussies over the years.

Recently the games have been a lot cleaner. I'm not sure if it has improved the game as a spectacle, as it was great to watch when there were a few fisticuffs. What GAA man doesn't love a good on-field row every now and again!

To be fair to the Irish teams, they never shied away from it. And this is especially true of Kieran McGeeney of Armagh. An Aussie was pulling and dragging out of him in one game, and McGeeney had had enough of his shite, so he took off his gloves, stared into the Aussie's eyes and gave him a look you'd give a man who knocked over your drink in a nightclub, as much as to say, 'Do you want to play football or do you want to fight me?' The big Aussie quickly got on with the match after that—no messing with the man who guided Armagh to their only Sam Maguire to date.

I hope the series continues, because it's a great chance for county stars to play with each other on the field and to have a few pints and a bit of craic with each other off it.

November

November on the GAA front is one of the quietest times of the year. The inter-county scene is well and truly over, and the club scene is at the provincial knockout stages. So, very little action takes place on the field.

Still, given the standard that the GAA is at these days, plenty of clubs will have appointed new and over-enthusiastic managers who will already be preparing for the following year. These fellas are full of beans: gym programmes, bleep tests, fat tests—you name it. November should always be the month when every GAA player can relax, have a few pints and not be ashamed of ordering a pizza for themselves.

'Yeah, and, sorry, can I have a bottle of Coke and an extra garlic dip, please? And how much is it for the biscuits ...?'

I suppose it's the time of year when the older lads, over a few pints in the local, might talk about retiring. You know, the same lad who's been retiring for the past five or six years.

'So, what d'you think, Mark: will you retire this year?'

'Ah, God, yeah. The knees are about to give in, and herself is always on to me about never being around.'

'Ah, will ya stop! Sure you've said you're retiring this past five years, and you'll still be the first man signing the attendance sheet at the meeting next January!'

'No, no, honestly, I'm done this year. I've had enough of that manager. I think I only played about forty-five minutes in total last year.'

'Well, to be fair, Mark, you are thirty-nine.'

'I am, but I'm a fucking fit man for thirty-nine.'

'I guarantee ya, we will see your bony hole at training next year, giving out to the young fellas because they're roasting ya.'

'No, ya won't. I'm done.'

There's a very good chance that Mark will be back at training the following January. I think every club can name at least three lads who should have retired but won't. You see, they can't break away from the scenery. People think it's the playing you miss, but in fact it's not: it's the slagging and banter that goes on within the dressing-room. That's what everyone really misses.

You can walk into any dressing-room and you'll find characters. Sure the banter over shower gel says it all: three-quarters of them don't bother bringing it any more, because once you flash a fresh shower gel in a dressing-room it'll be passed around quicker than the water bottles on a scorching evening.

I think the older fellas find it tough to throw in the towel because they live off stories from the young lads. The older bucks on the team do be always dying to hear the craic and scandal the young lads get up to after a great win in the championship.

'Boy Skinner, did yiz head out after the game last Saturday?'

'We did, yeah—ended up in Copper's till about five, then had a sing-song in Babylon after—some messing.'

'G'wan, tell us the craic. Had ya any luck with the women in Copper's?'

'I had, yeah.'

'Good man yourself. Did ya tell them about that run-out you got with the county last year?'

'I did indeed—had the photo saved on the phone of me kicking that free. Showed her and it worked a treat.'

'Ha! You're some buck. Where was she from?'

'Not sure, to be honest—was either Wexford, Waterford or Wicklow. Anyway, couldn't really hear: music was blaring.'

'Ah, to be nineteen again!'

So when any player retires, it's far more than the winning matches and the keeping fit that they miss the most: it's the tales of the younger brigade!

The Dinner Dance

GAA Dinner Dances are an old tradition taking place in the off-season, and they're a chance for a lot of club members to get together and have a shindig. They're generally for clubs celebrating a championship success, but many clubs hold them as mini-fundraisers and to celebrate all the achievements in the club. Truth be told, current players hate the sight of Dinner Dances, because it's a chance for the auld die-hards in the club to corner them at the bar and give them all sorts of abuse about why they didn't win this game or that.

'All I'm saying to ya is we should have won that game. Jaysus, it still haunts me thinking about it, and ya know how much I hate losing to them shower ...'

'I know, Fergal, I know. Listen, I'm going to head back over to the lads now...'

'C'mere, c'mere, JP, don't be getting annoyed now. I'm just telling ya that ya should have went for the goal: we'd have won then, no bother.'

'Fergal, I know, you've told me enough times. Listen, I'll chat to ya later.'

As JP is walking off, Fergal will turn to another sneerer who's impossible to please and say, 'That's what's wrong with these young lads, Peter—can't take a bit of criticism!'

The Dinner Dances can be good for the future of the club, though, as there's always a chance that, say, the son of a former sticky corner-back and the daughter of a former stylish corner-forward might end the night heading up to the far dugout, and you have a potential right good prospect on your hands in twenty years' time.

*

At every Dinner Dance they announce the award for the club's person of the year, which in 99 per cent of clubs is the most political decision you're likely to come across. You'll have poor Jimbob out breaking his bollox cutting the grass and cleaning out the changing-rooms every day, no questions asked—he just gets on with his work. You'd like to think he's in with a great shout of getting the award, but no chance. You have to be someone within the clique or 'circle' every GAA club has in order to receive this award.

December

There's not much happening on the playing front in the merry month of December. It's the time of year when the rumours float round about who the new manager for the following year will be.

'Did ya hear who's taking over?'

'No, who?'

'Y'know, your man who managed the grasshoppers to the junior A title two years ago.'

'Eh, Tony, is it?'

'Yep. I overheard Mary and Éamonn talking about it in the chipper Friday night.'

'Aw, Jaysus. A few lads I know from that club were telling me he's old school. He has this motto: every player should get sick at least once during the heavy running in January. He reckons if ya don't get sick you're not working hard enough. Meant to be a nut-job altogether.'

'Well, that's what the club needs: we weren't fit enough last year!'

*

No matter what happens in a match, the theory in the GAA is: 'If you're beat, you simply aren't fit enough.' I don't know what it is about GAA managers, but the more matches you win, the more ball you'll see at training; and the more matches you lose, the more you'll have the legs off ya at training.

You'll have had a great battle against an opposing team, but they completely rob you with a last-minute goal. After the game, the manager won't accept that you were just pure unlucky in conceding a scuttery last-minute soft goal, which should have been a free-out: he'll blame it on the team's fitness. The following Tuesday night, before training, he'll be sure to make the point.

'Men, we know we had that game won last Sunday. We had a two-point lead, and, as you know, a two-point lead is the most dangerous lead on a football field. We simply weren't fit enough, so I'm afraid we're going to have to up the runs in training ...'

The top 5 things GAA managers will blame a loss on after the game:

- We weren't fit enough.
- We weren't fit enough.
- We weren't fit enough.
- We weren't fit enough.
- We weren't fit enough.

County trials

Everyone remembers county trials. These generally take place in December. The trials, in which county teams try to unearth a hidden talent, aren't really that popular any more, except at the underage level. I'm not surprised: they were always tough.

A lot of people will remember going to underage county trials with a buddy from their club. You rock down, and nobody knows each other, so nobody passes the ball. Everyone is glory-hunting left, right and centre, so very good prospects are often overlooked. From under-12 to under-16 the strongest lads just play among themselves at the trials. You'll have a budding Colm Cooper stuck in corner-forward, the jersey swimming on him. The poor chap just stands there, with bundles of hidden talent, and players simply look at him and say to themselves, 'Size of that little fella in the corner— won't be kicking the ball near him!'

So it's very hard for these lads to stand out in underage trials, and many a good young player has no doubt fallen through the cracks.

At senior level now they just bring in three or four lads to play an in-house match in order to see if they're up to standard, watching them play with and against the best of the best that the county has to offer.

*

I had my own in-house 'trial match' with the senior county team back in 2008. It's a story I couldn't leave out of this book.

I was always very big for my age: my manager from under-10 to under-14 had to bring a copy of my birth cert to most matches to prove to the ref and the other team's manager that I wasn't a 'banger'.

From under-14 almost to minor football I had it all my own way. If I'm being honest, I was never a great footballer. I was the type of chap who, once I'd won a ball around midfield, would hear, 'Lay it off, Rory, lay it off,' from the sideline. I could catch most kick-outs, though, because I was a foot taller than anyone around me. I thought that the game was a 'piece of piss' and that I was destined for Croker!

Eventually, though, everyone around me began to grow naturally, and I wasn't as influential on the pitch as in my underage days.

Well, back in 2008 I was midfield for the Meath under-21 team. We got absolutely spanked by Kildare in championship in Navan. I did, though, have one of my better outings, and I was proud enough of my efforts.

In the showers after, we, like most GAA lads, tried to forget about the game and spoke instead about the drinking session we were going to go on. ''Mon we hit Navan, lads—drown the sorrows.'

As we headed back into the changing-rooms, Colm Coyle (then the Meath senior manager) called me over and says, 'I want you to come in for a training match tomorrow morning with the seniors. You deserve a shot after that performance.'

This was great news, but I was still mad for a few pints with the lads, as it was my last year at under-21. So I told them I'd go for the infamous 'one or two'.

Sure of course the craic was ninety, and as the night wore on I'd look in the mirror while washing my hands: you know the stare and conversation you give yourself after a few too many pints, just to try and justify your actions. 'Sure even if I play a stormer tomorrow, I'm still not going to be on the championship panel come June, so fuck it. I'll just arrive up and do my best'—a woeful attitude altogether. So I ended up getting absolutely locked and taking a taxi back to Ashbourne at about four in the morning, mouldy drunk!

The next morning I woke up on my couch in an awful heap. I heard the doorbell ring. The mother answered it and then came into the back room, saying, 'Cormac is at the door.' This was Cormac McGill, a fellow-clubman on the Meath team at the time.

'What does he want?' says I.

'You have a game, don't you?'

'Oh, *shite*, I do!'

So I jumped in the car, still in the jeans and shirt from the night before, stinking of drink.

'Where's your gear?' asked one of the lads in the back seat.

'Aw, boys, I can't play. I'm in an awful state. I wouldn't run up the stairs right now. I'll just say one of the Skryne lads was meant to pick it up for me and they forgot.' Such a brutal excuse!

So we got to the pitch—late, of course. Most of the panel were out on the field warming up. I'd got sick out the window on the way down to Navan, so I was as white as a ghost getting out of the car. Tommy Dowd, the Meath legend, who was a selector at the time, takes one look at me and says in a pure Co. Meath accent, 'You're *some* cowboy, O'Connor,' and burst out laughing.

I strutted into the changing-room, the entry stamp from the nightclub clearly visible on my hand, and stuttered my woeful excuse to a dead-wise Colm Coyle. I thought that, being size thirteen in boots, I'd have been safe enough and that nobody would have spare boots of that calibre, so I was thinking I was going to be sitting in the dugout, having the bit of craic during the game and letting my hangover pass by comfortably.

But no. Just my luck: an excited Mark Ward (then a Meath midfielder, and a man I'd had many a battle with in club games) piped up. 'Jaysus, Rory, I have a spare pair of thirteens in my bag here. You can wear them!' he knowing well the state I was in—the bollix!

'Ah, Jaysus, thanks, Wardy. You're such a gentleman!' I got a pair of socks and size-34 shorts off another lad. I'm size 38, at best, so they were completely bet onto me!

So off I headed onto the pitch to join the warm-up, looking like a chap they'd dragged in off the street in order to make up the numbers. I was marking Nigel Crawford (the Meath midfielder and all-Ireland winner), and I never got such a roasting in all my life. I was calling for kick-outs and jumping about ten seconds too early. The game was a complete disaster and an utter blur. Still to this day I couldn't tell you anything that happened in the first half!

After the game, as we were warming down by jogging from sideline to sideline, I had to pull up along the railings and put the fingers down the throat. I had done my best to hold it in, but, no, it was en route, and that was it. Anthony Moyles (the Meath captain at the time) walked by with a look of utter disgust on his face. He shook his head and pointed at me, saying, 'That is what is wrong with Meath football, right there.' I was in such a heap, down on my hunkers, that I couldn't even feel ashamed: I just stuck the fingers back down the throat again to get the last of the Navan Supermac's out of my system.

When I was eventually finished I didn't even bother having a shower: I just jumped into Cormac's car, sitting there dirty and freezing, waiting on the lads to come out so we could get the hell home.

To tell you the truth, I wasn't too surprised that I didn't get a call back to training the following Tuesday—nor to play another game for the Royal County! I'm sure there are plenty of folk around the country with their own county trial disaster. No doubt about it!

GAA legends

My top 5 legends

I want to highlight some of the legends of the GAA—people I would consider real heroes and icons of the game. When I sat down to try and pick five it wasn't easy, to say the least. There are so many people left out who have given so much, who have entertained us and made so many people happy over the years. And this is just the people on the national stage: you know as well as I do the number of great people in each and every GAA club all around the country—the people who go unnoticed but who put so much effort into making their GAA club an all-round better place. These folk make the GAA, in my eyes.

For as long as the GAA has been around it has been littered with real characters—people not afraid to speak their mind or to be true to themselves. I worry a bit about how serious everything is nowadays, with both players and managers afraid to give their honest opinion.

Some of the characters in our games have been incredible people. There's an endless number of legends, past and present, who make the GAA what it is. But here, in no order, is my top 5.

1. Páidí Ó Sé (An Ghaeltacht and Kerry)

The Kerry icon Páidí Ó Sé—what a man. I visited his home only this year (2017). It's in Ventry, Co. Kerry—a fabulous place. I was down in Dingle for the night and tipped out to PO's for a couple of pints of black.

You could spend an hour walking around his pub, looking at the many people whose lives he touched in one way or another. His son Pádraig Óg, a sound young man, showed me around. There are some iconic photos of past and present legends of the game going toe to toe. He even managed to get Tom Cruise in behind the bar to pull a pint!

One regret I have is that I never got to meet Páidí in the flesh. What a character. The stories about the fiery wing-back that circle around are unreal—a wild hoor, by all accounts. He knew how to go hard, both on and off the field.

Outside his pub there's a statue of him in his beloved green-and-gold kit of Kerry. His list of honours, as both player and manager, is on the wall behind him. My God, what a list of achievements in his short fifty-seven years walking this earth. Most of us would settle for one county medal, never mind an all-Ireland cross. Well, this man had them coming from all angles and out of every pocket. I was amazed at how much success he had.

I've listed his credentials below, in case you weren't already aware of them. Bear in mind that these are just the major honours: he has won plenty more.

Player

- 8 all-Ireland senior medals;
- 11 Munster senior medals;
- 4 National Football League medals;
- 4 Railway Cups;
- 2 Kerry county medals.

Manager

- 2 all-Ireland senior championships;
- 6 Munster senior championships;
- 1 all-Ireland under-21 championship;
- 2 Munster under-21 championships;
- 1 National Football League;
- 3 county senior championships;
- 1 Leinster senior football championship (Westmeath).

I've watched the RTÉ documentary *Marooned* a couple of times—a great insight into the nature of the man. My God, he lived for football. Something he said during the programme, as he carried a football along the beaches of west Co. Kerry, sums up his passion for the game. 'When I wake up in the morning, the first thing I think about is football and Kerry, and the last thing I think about before I go to bed at night is Kerry and football.'

He was a real dog on the football pitch. Of course, I was too young to see him in action, but I've watched many a tape of him and that great Kerry team of the 70s, littered with incredible talent: Jack O'Shea, Mikey Sheehy, Eoin 'Bomber' Liston and the evergreen Pat Spillane, to name just a few. They were leaders and winners!

There's a classic clip of Páidí trying to tackle Cork's Dinny Allen from behind. Dinny, clearly not happy with PO's aggressive nature, swings an elbow that catches Páidí right on the puss. PO takes a split second to make sure his jaw is still intact, and takes another split second to make up his mind what he'll do. Then *bang*! As good a left hook as you'll ever see. In thunders the referee to calm matters, but he slips and lands on his arse—a classic bit of GAA footage. If there was one man who wasn't going to turn to the ref to ask him to show Dinny a card for a wild elbow it was Páidí: he was more than happy to take matters into his own hands, and, by God, he did!

He managed Westmeath to victory in the Leinster championship in 2004, which was their one and only. That was some achievement—the famous helicopter journeys from Co. Kerry to Mullingar for training. The RTÉ documentary gives us a great insight into this new phase of Páidí's career and into his sheer passion for the team to succeed. In it he gives one of the greatest GAA speeches ever to have been recorded—a real classic. He pitched this to the Westmeath team after their drawn Leinster final in 2004. There was going to be only one winner in the replay, after this speech. Just try and read it without hearing it in PO's Kerry accent!

*

We're going well, lads. But, lads, bring the bit of fucking divilment into your play the next day now, and the tigerish play, the discipline, the tightness, the rough-and-tumble stuff out around the middle of the field, the fucking breaking ball.

A grain of rice is going to tip the scale. Just remember that, lads: a grain of rice will tip the scale. But you'll have to get steely tough upstairs, and you must be willing to fucking break your gut.

You were fucked over the line twice—fucked over the line like you'd catch a fucking loaf of bread, and fuck you over the line with his shoulder. And what that does is it lifts the opposition.

We don't want to see no Westmeath man fucked about. Is that clear now, Alan? No more! You'll have to be closer: closer ta fuck.

We'll have to fucking crash into these fellas and test out their fucking pulse, because I'm telling ye, lads, these fellas will play good football if they're allowed.

Give me one fucking guarantee, each and every one of you, that ye're going to be tighter, that ye're going to be more disciplined, that ye're going to be more tigerish, and that ye're going to take the fucking game to these fellas—that these fellas will get such a fucking shell-shock next Saturday evening that we'll put them back on their fucking arses for fucking ten years.

*

Now if that speech doesn't have you running through walls, nothing will. There's no doubt that everyone who met Páidí Ó Sé has their own unique story about him—a true Gael and a complete icon of the GAA.

Rest in peace, PO.

2. Cora Staunton (Carnacon and Mayo)

I've been saying it for years: women footballers and camogie players simply don't get the recognition they deserve, and some incredible players have come and gone over the years. Briege Corkery, Juliet Murphy and Valerie Mulcahy of Cork; Mags D'Arcy of Wexford; Angela Downey of Kilkenny; and Therese Maher of Galway, to name but a few.

CORA
STAUNTON

I suppose nobody sticks out in my mind more than Mayo's legendary player Cora Staunton. This woman is just an outrageous talent and has been playing for the Mayo senior team since she was thirteen years of age ... *Thirteen!*

She is presently (2017) still leading the Mayo attack at the ripe age of thirty-four. That is twenty-one years playing at the top level—just unheard of. The fact that she keeps coming back, year after year, and is maintaining her performance at the highest level is outstanding.

Her mantelpiece at home must be bursting with honours. This is what she has achieved to date:

- 4 all-Ireland senior championship medals;
- 3 National Football League medals;
- 5 all-Ireland club medals with Carnacon (and more than a dozen Mayo county championships);
- 10 All-Star awards.

In the 2016 club campaign Staunton scored 9-12 in a club game and went on to kick 1-15 in the Connacht final. These are scoring tallies you wouldn't see at an under-12 blitz, never mind a provincial club final! I've seen her play on many occasions, and she's just top class—a scoring machine—and I'm sure anyone who has marked her will tell you the same.

She's the type of player who gets fouled more often than not, simply because people can't handle her skill and strength as she comes at you. Oh, how the Mayo senior men's team could have done with a Cora Staunton over the past twenty years: there would be no whisper of a curse then. The Sam Maguire would have visited the grass of Belmullet at least once, that's for sure!

Staunton has also had some success playing soccer with Ballyglass Ladies and, in rugby, with Castlebar Ladies. She's a truly outstanding talent—without a shadow of a doubt the greatest women's footballer of all time, and a true inspiration for any girl aiming to reach the top of her sport.

3. Brian Cody (James Stephens and Kilkenny)

When you think of the game of hurling, together with the word 'manager', not too many people come into your head other than Brian Cody. What a servant to the game of hurling and to the county of Kilkenny. He's very much an Alex Ferguson type of character—a born winner.

Brian is a figure very easily identified on the sideline: he always stands there with the arms folded, observing the action, and spitting on the hands when he gets excited. And the Glanbia baseball cap on him, which he's had since the 90s. God help the linesman if he gives an incorrect decision against the Cats.

'Calm down, Brian. Please stand away from the field, Brian. Calm down.'

Any Kilkenny player will tell you how driven for success the man is. There's no half-arsed commitment under the James Stephens clubman: you are either in or you are out.

Everyone has heard of the infamous A v. B matches the Kilkenny panel had during their dominance in the 2000s. The word on the street is that Brian blew the whistle three times in the hour: once to start the game, a second time to call for the ball at half time and the third and final time when he was satisfied that they had beaten the complete shite out of each other enough. When he starts the game I think he must put the whistle deep down into his pocket, clearly suggesting to the players, 'Listen, fellas, this is a licence to take the shins and fingers off each other here today. If a row breaks out, a row breaks out. Just leave the helmets on ye.'

These games were meant to be 'hair and skin flying' battles. I can imagine the likes of JJ Delaney taking the head off Eddie Brennan in many a game, and Brian standing there spitting on the hands, delighted with what he was witnessing.

Brian was a hugely successful player for Kilkenny, manning the full-back line with a no-nonsense approach. His collection of honours, as both player and manager, speaks for itself.

Player

- 3 all-Ireland senior championship medals;
- 4 Leinster senior championship medals;
- 2 National Hurling League medals;
- 2 all-Ireland under-21s championship medals;
- 2 Leinster under-21s championship medals;
- 1 all-Ireland minor championship medal;
- 2 Leinster minor championship medals;
- 2 All-Star awards.

Manager

- 11 all-Ireland senior championships;
- 15 Leinster senior championships;
- 8 National Hurling Leagues.

Brian is a hugely successful and respected man, and it won't be long before there's a statue of him on the streets of Kilkenny.

4. Mícheál Ó Muircheartaigh (Dingle and Kerry)

There have been some great GAA commentators. You can go back to the original king of commentary, Michael O'Hehir, who my father often spoke about. Listening to O'Hehir on the wireless was his earliest memory of GAA matches, the whole family gathered round in the living-room as O'Hehir described every last inch of play. He made you feel as if you were sitting in the middle of the Hogan Stand watching the match. This scene, of a family gathering round to listen to matches, is one many older GAA folk will recall with fondness.

These days you have the likes of Marty Morrissey, Ger Canning and Darragh Maloney —all fantastic commentators who can have you on the edge of your seat for matches, both on the TV and on the radio.

'Seán Óg Ó hAilpín: his father's from Fermanagh, his mother's from Fiji. Neither a hurling stronghold.'

MÍCHEÁL
O' MUIRCHEARTAIGH

But it's fair to say that, among commentators, the cream of the crop is the great Mícheál Ó Muircheartaigh. Whatever it is about his soft Kerry voice, it is just compelling. He could make two flies landing on a cow pat sound exciting: he just has this amazing knack with words. Some of his famous sayings in commentary are top class. Below are some favourites. There are not too many GAA people who won't have heard them. They are just classic.

*

'Seán Óg Ó hAilpín: his father's from Fermanagh; his mother's from Fiji. Neither a hurling stronghold.'

'... and Brian Dooher is down injured. And, while he is, I'll tell ye a little story. I was in Times Square in New York last week, and I was missing the championship back home. So I approached a newsstand, and I said, "I suppose ye wouldn't have The Kerryman, would ye?" To which the Egyptian behind the counter turned to me and he said, "Do you want the north Kerry edition or the south Kerry edition?" He had both—so I bought both. And Dooher is back on his feet ...'

'Colin Corkery on the 45 lets go with the right boot. It's over the bar. This man shouldn't be *playing football: he's made an almost Lazarus-like recovery from a heart condition. Lazarus was a great man, but he couldn't kick points like Colin Corkery.'*

'Teddy McCarthy to Mick McCarthy, no relation. Mick McCarthy back to Teddy McCarthy, still no relation.'

'I saw a few Sligo people at Mass in Gardiner Street this morning, and the omens seem to be good for them: the priest was wearing the same colours as the Sligo jersey! Forty yards out on the Hogan Stand side of the field, Ciarán Whelan goes on a rampage ... It's a goal! So much for religion.'

'Pat Fox has it on his hurl and is motoring well now, but here comes Joe Rabbitte hot on his tail ... I've seen it all now: a Rabbitte chasing a Fox around Croke Park!'

*

I have met Mícheál on a couple of occasions and found him as much a gentleman as you would imagine. He hosted the launch of my uncle's book, *County Kerry: 101 Interesting Facts*, and his speech was amazing. His knowledge of everything Kerry and GAA is incredible. You could listen to him all night.

I offered to buy him a drink after, but he was heading off to another function with his wife, so he had no time to hang around and have me waffle the ears off him. I suppose everyone wanted to be in Mícheál's company and hear his stories and experiences.

He's known as 'the voice of Gaelic games'. No better man fits this bill. A legend.

5. Seán Boylan (Dunboyne and Meath)

There have been many legendary managers in the GAA. You have the likes of Brian Cody: on paper, head and shoulders the most successful manager the GAA has ever seen. You have Mick O'Dwyer, who managed the famous Kerry team of the 1970s, widely regarded as the greatest football team of all time. You have Mickey Harte of Tyrone, the man who guided the red-hand county to all three of their all-Ireland successes. At the time of writing, he's still at the helm, and doing a very decent job, at that. Jim Gavin must also get a mention for his success with Dublin in recent times.

But, being a Meath man, I'll have to be a bit biased here and talk about the great Seán Boylan, the man who guided the Royal County to no fewer than four Sam Maguire Cups.

Anyone who has ever met Seán will know what I mean when I say he has this charisma about him—a very bubbly man. I often wonder how a man as nice as he is could rein in the likes of Mick Lyons, Gerry McEntee and Graham Geraghty in the dressing-room, but, by Jaysus, he did, and did it in style.

*

That great Meath team of the 1980s were probably the first to bring a bit of 'dirt' into the game, and I don't mean that in a bad way: I mean they played on the edge and earned the reputation of being the 'hard men' of the GAA.

Bernard Flynn, a fantastic corner-forward in his day, and a man whose company I enjoy, has told a great story of his early days in the Meath set-up. He was marking the very imposing and intimidating Mick Lyons in a trial match. Lyons, being Lyons, was throwing his weight around. This is how Flynn described what followed.

'Mick Lyons was on me. I was very young at the time, maybe twenty-two. The first ball, he hit me hard into the ribs. I told him, "Don't fucking do that again, Mick, I fucking mean it." But I was shitting myself. The next ball, he went right through me, and after I got up I hit him again. I knew I was being tested. In my mind, I had to hit him to earn the respect of the group. So I drove him in the face as hard as I could. I split his nose straight down the middle, down to the white. The blood came pumping out. He didn't even go down—just stood there, shook his head and started wiping the blood away. Boylan was refereeing and didn't blink—just let it go.'

Lyons approached Flynner after the match. He was full sure that Lyons was going to take a swipe at him, but instead Lyons put his arm around his shoulder, looked him straight in the eye and said, 'That's the stuff, Bernie. It's more of that we want here.'

*

That's one of the many stories to come out of that Meath camp during them glory years. Seán had won two all-Irelands with that bunch of hardy boyos.

Meath hit a dip in the early 90s, before coming back with another crop of talent, landing two more all-Ireland crosses, in 1996 and 1999.

Unfortunately, from my biased Meath point of view, that was as good as it got for the time being, but Seán was key to those successes. Any player I've ever spoken to who worked under Seán said he had amazing man-management skills. He made fellas feel and think that they were better than they actually were. He got the most out of them, making an average fella great.

And this was true no more so than for Big John McDermott—an icon of mine, growing up. He was what you'd call an average footballer, but Seán shaped him into one of the best midfielders of his generation—a real workhorse. Big John Mac played to a system where he just had to do his job and let the likes of Trevor Giles, Ollie Murphy and Tommy Dowd worry about the flashy stuff. He just made sure he dominated his sector of the field and moved the ball on as soon as he could.

Here's hoping that Meath can go back to near their glory days in the coming years. It will take something special to create the buzz in the county that Seán managed to create in the 80s and 90s. He's a man who'll be remembered around the hills of Tara till the end of time.

My top 5 footballers

Everyone has their favourite players, and nobody is right or wrong: so many hugely talented footballers have played the game. I've picked my top 5 for my generation (1997–2017). It wasn't easy, and so many greats have been left out. These players I have been in awe of over the years—sheer greats of their generation.

1. Darragh Ó Sé (An Ghaeltacht and Kerry)

Darragh is the best midfielder of all time, in my opinion. He had everything in his locker that it took to be an outstanding number 8. He wasn't the biggest man ever to wrestle around midfield, but what he had was perfect timing. He could hang for what seemed like minutes and pluck the ball from the sky at his highest peak—a real salmon jumping from the water.

He was a brilliant foot-passer and always looked for the kick-pass into the full-forward line in possession. He had that edge to him as well and wasn't afraid to rumble with you when he had to.

Himself and his two brothers, Tomás and Marc, were as good as any players of their time. No surprise when their uncle went by the name of Páidí!

There aren't enough compliments for Darragh. All I can add is that he was my favourite of the three legendary brothers from Ventry, and that his honours on the field of play speak for themselves.

2. Peter Canavan (Errigal Ciarán and Tyrone)

There's an old saying: 'It's not the size of the dog in the fight; it's the size of the fight in the dog,' and nobody fits that bill more than Wee Peter Canavan. He's a small man but a monster in the effect he had on any game he played in.

The harder full-backs tried to take the head off him, the more he rose in the game. He was like an elastic band as he jumped, hopped and skipped round defenders of all shapes and sizes. He played on Tyrone teams looking like the only man on the field, and no more so than in the all-Ireland final of 1995, when he kicked ten points against the Dubs and still ended up on the losing team.

I believe there's very little between himself and the Gooch as regards being the greatest forward of all time. The Gooch is fresher in people's minds, but Canavan is right up there with him, in my opinion.

Now, before you eat the head off me, go onto YouTube and watch the five-minute clip called 'Peter Canavan: club scores.' I'll leave this one there. 'Peter the Great' is right.

3. Colm Cooper (Dr Crokes and Kerry)

Well, this was an easy decision. What more can be said about the Gooch, only that he was a wizard. He hung up his boots this year (2017), and the tributes that poured in show just how highly regarded he is.

What everyone loves about him is his natural ability on the ball; his vision and his execution of a foot-pass were just top notch. You can do all the weights and fitness training you want, but you can't buy what Cooper has. Sheer class.

He arrived on the scene looking like what can only be described as a chap who hadn't had a good dinner in months—the old-fashioned baggy jersey hanging over him. I'd say many a corner-back looked at him and laughed as they shook hands, thinking this was going to be a handy day at the office. Big mistake, because once this man got the ball in his hands, a genius was at work.

It was always hard to figure out which was his stronger foot, as he kicked points and scored many great goals off either foot with such ease. Finishing off your last playing day in Croke Park by winning an all-Ireland with your club—could you dream of anything better? It was a fitting way for a true great to end his days, in the theatre of dreams.

What a master with an O'Neill's in hand. He will go down as one of the greatest footballers of all time, if not *the* greatest.

4. Seán Cavanagh (Moy and Tyrone)

How good a player is this man! Midfield or full-forward, this fella is going to do a job for ya. I would rank him up there with any player, during any era. A serious competitor—relentless every time he plays and with a never-say-die attitude.

Tell me this, how many lads have fallen for his famous 'shimmy-dummy' over the years? The man marking him, the rest of the players on the field, the whole stand and everyone watching on TV know it's coming, but it seems to work every time. As his opponent is lining him up he says to himself, 'Right, he's defo going to do his shimmy. Don't dive in, don't dive in, it's coming, don't dive in ... Ah, *shite*,' as Seán skips by his man and clips over yet another score for the red-hand county.

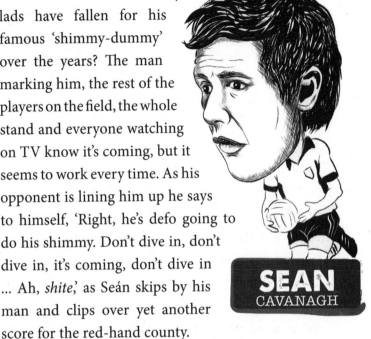

SEAN
CAVANAGH

How many times have you seen him burst through defences and have the brains to fist-pass over the bar as the keeper comes bearing down on him? Then he trots back out to midfield, not a bother on him.

He's one man I would have hated to mark in his prime. A machine for running up and down the field, and he has a serious football vision to direct him into the right place at the right time.

Such a key man for Tyrone, he only hung up the boots in 2017, after serving his county for fifteen years. Seán was outstanding. An all-time great footballer.

5. Trevor Giles (Skryne and Meath)

What a class act this man is. For a long time, every young lad in Meath wanted to be him, including myself. His vision in possession was unreal; his free-taking off the deck was a joy to watch; and the way he'd send the ball off out to the right, letting it curl back in over the black spot, was incredible. A very unassuming man, still to this day.

I've played against him many a time at club level, and he'd go about his business in such a respectful manner. He'd never get involved in any bullshit on the pitch. He has no time for hand-cuffs or sledging: he's just there to play the game and to play it with style and swagger.

I remember being at a club game in which Trevor was hitting a free from about forty yards. The man he was marking was roaring at him, 'Go on, Trevor, kick it with your left, there, if you're as good as you think you are.' Trevor placed the ball down, turned on his left and kicked it straight over the bar. He didn't say a word or make a gesture to his man: he just jogged back into position. That was Giles all over—just gets on with the game.

He's a real Meath legend and a man who has the honour of being the only player to win two Player of the Year awards, in 1996 and 1999. Oh, how Meath could do with him nowadays!

My top 5 hurlers

There have been so many top-class hurlers over the years, which makes selecting a top 5 a very tough job. After much consideration, and plenty of cups of coffee, I went for the following players.

1. Tommy Walsh (Tullaroan and Kilkenny)

The first choice was one of the easiest decisions I've had to make. What a hurler this man was: small in stature but a complete beast of a fella on the field. The term 'dog' is thrown around a lot in the GAA, and some people might not recognise it as praise: if someone on the field was to call you a dog it's a big compliment, and no greater dog has graced a GAA field than the bould Tommy Walsh.

I'm not sure if there was ever a better man for catching a sliotar. He used to rise above any fella, getting a kick-start off the back of his heel and another lift off his backside, and he'd leap over his shoulder and pluck the sliotar.

'Puck the shagging ball anywhere, except down on top of Tommy Walsh.' How many keepers over the years have had that roared at them from the sideline during a big championship match? That's how good Tommy was.

It's a reflection of the influence he had on games that Tipperary felt they needed to have one of their marquee forwards, Lar Corbett, follow him all over the field to try and keep him out of the game. Bizarre tactics, to say the least!

Tommy has won nine All-Stars in a row, in five different positions. We will *never* see that done again. He's a very unassuming man, and that's what makes him such hero, not just to the people of Kilkenny but to all GAA people throughout the world. The great Tommy Walsh from Tullaroan.

2. Henry Shefflin (Ballyhale Shamrocks and Kilkenny)

There have been so many outstanding talents to have held a bit of ash timber in their paws. You have the likes of Eddie Keher, DJ Carey and Eddie Brennan of Kilkenny; Christy Ring of Cork; Eoin Kelly and Nicky English of Tipperary; Ken McGrath, John Mullane and Tony Browne of Waterford; Brian Lohan and Jamesie O'Connor of Clare; and Brian Whelahan and Johnny Dooley of Offaly, among many others. But I don't think anyone can argue with the fact that Henry Shefflin was the greatest of them all.

HENRY SHEFFLIN

When you think medals in the game, nobody comes close to 'King Henry'. He's the man in the GAA when it comes to honours. Whenever Kilkenny—or Ballyhale, for that matter—needed a player to stand up when the game was in the cauldron, it was Henry who often took control of the game. Ever so reliable with frees—and with penalties, when they needed to be put away at a crucial moment in the match—Shefflin would step up to rattle the onion sack time and time again.

Most players might enjoy a few pints and a chipper after winning a big game, but Henry's idea of celebrating was to have a cup of tea and a chocolate biscuit: that's the level of commitment he had!

I could write a whole book on Henry's career, but I'll simply finish by saying that he's the greatest. Nothing sums the man up better than that.

3. John Mullane (De La Salle and Waterford)

I'd love to know what work-out protein John Mullane took on board before Munster championship matches. The king of fist-pumps, Mullane was hard not to love when he was playing hurling. He wore his heart on his sleeve in every game, and he was wired to the moon. The better he was playing, the more electricity flowed through his body.

That interview he gave after a Munster championship match, with the Waterford people behind him! 'I just love me county so much, and the people of Waterford.' Straight from the heart—no bullshit with Mullane.

He was like an ambassador for Vaseline during his heyday: he had layers of it over his bushy, sunburnt eyebrows. His trademark was to bring the sliotar out on the wing, take one look and smack it over his shoulder—straight over the black spot. Then he'd celebrate by grabbing the badge on his jersey and shaking his hurl in mid-air with excitement.

He was a real character of the sport, and, like I said, there are not too many like Mullane around any more. You just know the man is great craic on a night out, from the way he hurled. He won five All-Stars, and, given that Waterford reached only one final (2008) during his time, I think his individual haul of awards speaks volumes. A real favourite of the fans, he was a sheer bundle of energy and a man I don't think Waterford, or the GAA, will replace any time soon.

4. Diarmuid O'Sullivan (Cloyne and Cork)

You're probably wondering why the big man is in my top 5. He's certainly not the most talented hurler of all time, but I just loved the man on a hurling field—a big brute in the full-back line. He wouldn't have looked out of place playing Ivan Drago in *Rocky IV*. When Diarmuid caught a sliotar on the run and charged down the field, you may as well have been meeting a rhino head-on at forty miles an hour. 'The Rock' made many a man feel like a defenceless animal as they tried to stop him coming out with the sliotar.

Without question the greatest 'burst' I've ever seen was the Rock against Limerick in the 2001 Munster championship quarter-final. The ball was played into the Limerick full-

DIARMUID
O'SULLIVAN

forward line, and out charged O'Sullivan. He had gathered up that much momentum after collecting the sliotar that the Limerick man in front of him could have been an elephant, and he was still getting landed on his arse. Diarmuid had that much adrenaline pumping through him, from putting the Limerick man on his hole, that he took a ferocious swing at the sliotar. I'd imagine that it was to clear his lines, and that he would have been happy to have landed it in the full-forward line; but the big beast from Cloyne connected with it so well that it sailed over the bar from a ridiculous distance out the field. It's one of my favourite GAA moments. It's proof that when O'Sullivan takes the impact of a shoulder before pucking the sliotar, he can cover a distance of 150 yards with one swipe.

I'm sure he must have been a weightlifting world champion in a previous life. The Rock would be full-back on my team any day.

5. Ken McGrath (Mount Sion and Waterford)

One of my favourite hurlers of all time. You'd have him in your team all day long. A real leader of that great Waterford team I'd love to have seen win the Liam MacCarthy. How many games has Ken lorded it from half-back? Up would go the big paw to clamp the sliotar like a vice; he'd wiggle his way out of a crowd with his hand in the air, almost telling the ref, 'I have it, I have it. Give me my free.'

KEN McGRATH

The ref would wave play on, and McGrath would blast the ball straight back where it came from.

I have a lot of time for that Waterford team, with the likes of himself, Dan 'the Man' Shanahan, Michael 'Brick' Walsh, Tony Browne, John Mullane and Paul Flynn. They had such a passion for the game, and none more so than Ken. He was in his prime when helmets weren't required, and he lost one of his front teeth for his troubles. But did he put on a helmet in his next game? No chance!

In 2014 Ken went under the knife for open-heart surgery. Of course, being the warrior he is, he came through it with flying colours. He's a man I respect so much for everything he's given to his club, Mount Sion, to Co. Waterford and to the GAA in general. He represents everything that the association is about: heart, respect and commitment. A real hero.

Epilogue

I've really enjoyed writing this book and being able to show you how similar every GAA club is. The GAA is something I'm very passionate about: the number of relationships you develop through it is incredible, and it's something we as Irish people should be very proud of.

Go raibh míle maith agaibh.

Acknowledgements

I would like to take this opportunity to thank everyone who has made this book possible for me. All the team at Gill Books—Conor Nagle, Sarah Liddy, Catherine Gough and Ellen Monnelly. Jen Murphy (Jen Murphy Designs) for her brilliant work on all the illustrations. She captured the characters perfectly. My agent, David Anderson (Outset Agency) for all his guidance and advice. My right-hand man Paddy Murphy, for all his involvement and time invested in the videos. My close friends Colm Ó Méalóid and Cormac McGill, who were a great help along the way with their knowledge of all things GAA. My mother and father, Marie and Joe, who have always been so supportive of me and my mad ideas! My sister Carol for her confidence in me. My beautiful daughter Ella and, finally, my fiancée, Emma—the person who always believed in me. Thank you all.